liquididea press

Advance Praise for
Indie & Small Press Book Marketing

"Finally, a structured approach to marketing books."
— **Tonya Macalino**, author of *Spectre of Intention* and *The Shades of Venice*

"Even for the traditionally published author, this book is full of great stuff! It takes a detailed, easy to follow approach to promoting your book. Highly recommended!"
— **E.C. Ambrose**, author of *The Dark Apostle* series

"Too many authors say there isn't any way to market your ebook except to just write another. Will Hertling's story demonstrates there is another path and now he has put that path down in a book that is easy to execute and full of useful information."
— **Erik Wecks**, author of *Aetna Rising: A Snowball's Chance in Hell*

"Chock full of actionable marketing tips I wish I'd known years ago."
— **Gene Kim**, author of *The Visible Ops Handbook* and *The Phoenix Project: A Novel About IT, DevOps, and Helping Your Business Win* (itrevolution.com)

INDIE & SMALL PRESS
BOOK MARKETING

Indie & Small Press Book Marketing

William Hertling

liquididea press
Portland, Oregon

Keywords: self publishing, indie publishing, small press, publishing, marketing, book marketing, online marketing, author platform

Table of Contents

Introduction

In December, 2011, I independently published my first novel, *Avogadro Corp*. Three months later, I published my second novel, *A.I. Apocalypse*. By July 2012, I was selling more than two thousand books a month. I sold more than fifteen thousand books in my first year as an author.

These sales helped me achieve the #2 and #5 best-selling technothriller spots on Amazon, brought my income from royalties into the replacement-salary range, and helped me sign an agreement with a New York agent to pursue traditional publication and movie rights sales for my third novel.

By comparison, the average indie-published book sells less than two hundred copies over its entire life, while traditionally published first novels sell, on average, seven hundred and fifty books.

What made my books different? In a word: marketing.

To promote my books, I drew upon years of experience as a social networking strategist at a large technology company, employed user experience design principles and content optimization practices, and comprehensively studied what others did for book marketing.

While I tried nearly everything, I didn't do so blindly. I intensely experimented and tracked my results, finding what worked and what didn't. This allowed me to focus on what I should do more of.

I was able to drive initial sales, set up the conditions that enabled ongoing book purchases, and maximized my chances of landing a "big fish" (more on that later).

At the Willamette Writers Conference in Portland, agents, film producers, and fellow writers were amazed by my sales. Not only were agents interested in my success, they were pitching their agencies to me (instead of the other way around).

I found myself retelling the story of how I'd achieved these results dozens of times, including an impromptu presentation to a standing-room only crowd. As I did this, I realized I needed a better way to share what I'd done.

In this volume, I'll share my approach to book marketing. Unlike other titles on marketing, there are no sleazy tricks or promises of unrealistic achievements. It's a combination of methodical approach, traditional marketing principles, and continual experimentation.

The path I took can be divided into four phases:

1. **Pre-launch:** This is what I did while I was writing, editing, and designing my novel. Good marketing starts long before your book is available in the store. It includes establishing a social media and web presence, making effective title and cover design choices, and ensuring that your published work is of the best quality.

2. **Launch:** The moment of book release, a launch is a carefully planned set of activities designed to get initial sales and reviews that will set up the book for continued success. For our purposes, the launch will be a month long period that starts with the publication of your book and ends with a celebratory (but purposeful) launch party.

3. **Post-launch:** After the initial launch, it's necessary to monitor and use social networks and websites to engage existing and would-be readers, amplify positive mentions, and experiment with targeted advertising. This also covers

engaging with communities and using book giveaways to drive more sales.

4. **Landing Influencers (aka the Big Fish):** With all the conditions set up right, you'll turn the odds in your favor that an influencer with a large social network and reach will read your book. By managing the relationship well, you can turn a minor splash into a big event.

I can't promise that this is the best approach to book marketing or that it's guaranteed to work for all books for all people. There are undoubtedly other ways to sell books: Some people excel at in-person events such as book signings, conventions, and convincing small bookstore owners to carry their books. Others may have friendships with journalists or other media professionals they can utilize.

In my case, I played to my strengths. I have free time in the early mornings and late evenings, which is good for doing things online, and not so good for doing things in person. I'm comfortable writing, and find interacting with people online to be fun. I'm willing to try new web sites and experiment.

If this sounds at all like you, then this book is for you.

My strengths, combined with my experience in social media strategy, web design, and intensive study of how to market books led to this approach.

My basic philosophy is that selling books is like achieving flight in an airplane. An airplane taxiing down a runway must achieve a minimum takeoff speed or the plane will never achieve flight. Similarly, with hundreds of thousands of new books being published each year, it's necessary to rise above the noise level to get enough attention. Getting initial sales, reviews, and mentions are the equivalent to the minimum speed necessary for takeoff. Once there, it's possible to sustain sales.

If a new book doesn't hit those minimum thresholds, then sales will languish indefinitely.

The four phase approach I outline will set you up with the right tools and resources to get started, help you achieve a burst of initial sales to reach takeoff velocity, and then guide you on a course to maintain flight.

In this book I describe a plan that starts before you publish. However, you can still use this plan even if your book is already for sale. Simply ignore the portions about the mechanics of publishing and start as though you're launching your book for the first time.

I assume throughout this book that you may have a day job, a family, and other obligations, and that you are a one-person operation. If you are fortunate enough to be able to write full-time, or have help marketing, you'll naturally see certain topics that could be started earlier.

For example, if you blog and develop a following before you publish, you can use that following to help with the launch. If you engage with influencers now, you'll be able to better drive sales later.

But most of us don't live in that ideal world. That's part of the reason why I split activities among the different phases.

Read through the entire book once to get a feel for the overall process. Then focus on a single phase at a time, instead of trying to do everything at once. This will reduce overwhelm and increase your effectiveness.

Phase 1: Pre-Launch

Overview

The major goals during this first phase include:

1. A well-written book.
2. Search engine friendly title.
3. Professional quality cover and interior design for ereader and print formats.
4. Establish web presence and social media identity.
5. Create business cards.

Well-Written Book

It's an imperative that you have a well-written book for your target audience.

A fiction book will have a compelling plot, interesting characters, great dialogue and description. A non-fiction book will address the subject matter with well-organized content that helps the reader achieve the goals you've described.

In all cases, the text should be free from spelling and grammar errors, repetitive words or sentence structure, and anything else that detracts from the reader's experience. It's beyond the scope of this book to cover this topic in detail, but let me tell you a little about my journey.

In 2009, my employer changed their vacation policy, and I had to use all of my accumulated vacation before the end of the year or I'd lose it. So I took four weeks off work, wrote full-time, and completed the first draft of *Avogadro Corp*. When I was finished, at 27,000 words, I'd written a novella. I gave it to my spouse and a few friends to read, made some minor corrections, and thought I was ready to submit it to publishers.

I received several form rejections, and one very short but personalized rejection from the editor of Panverse Publishing. He said that he loved singularity stories, but that my story took place in a white room, devoid of any description. I valued that criticism because it gave me a direction to improve. I tried my best to add description: to share people's emotions, to talk about the environment, to convey more than just the bare bones of the story.

When I was done with this new draft, I wanted feedback from someone other than my friends and family. I shared the book with half a dozen people I knew through a programmer's group: people I thought would enjoy the book and be blunt with me. Only one read it and gave me feedback, which amounted to "Show, don't tell."

At this point I'd been working on *Avogadro Corp* for about seven months. What I thought was finished as a 27,000 word novella was now a 50,000 word short novel. But I didn't have the skills to know what to do with the "show, don't tell" feedback. So I registered for an eight-week writing class at The Attic Institute in Portland. Over the course of those weeks, I learned about writing scenes, dialogue, and emotion, book structure, and good writing habits. I took part in workshop critique, and ultimately, with several classmates, formed a critique group that continued to meet biweekly.

Three months later – a year from the time I started – I had a finished 67,000 word novel. In that time, I had gone through fourteen revisions of the novel, almost tripled the word count, and learned dozens of writing skills I simply didn't have before.

But I still wasn't done. Before *Avogadro Corp* was finally published, it went through two rounds of editing (one paid, one free) and paid proofreading.

Even after all of that, the final product was just borderline passable: there were still typographical and grammar errors, as well as repetitive word use and sentence structure.

Your experience will not be the same as mine. You may start off as a better writer, or have friends able to critique your work, or you may be a better editor of your work. But this story should give you a rough calibration of the significant effort and expertise needed to publish a quality written work. By the time your book is published, you should feel that you've had to stretch yourself to write and edit the best possible book.

Choosing a Title

You may have started your book with a notion of the final title. Or an idea may come to you while writing. Hopefully the title is evocative of the major premise of the book. Unfortunately, that alone is not enough.

Here are some of the characteristics you'll need in your title:

Search engine friendly: Enter your prospective title into Google and Amazon. Ideally, the title is unique enough that Google returns very few results and Amazon returns no results. The ideal is that the title is so unique that if you create a web page for your book, it will easily become the top search result in Google.

For *Avogadro Corp*, this was very easy. Avogadro's Number is a relatively famous term with many search results, but there were almost no results for "Avogadro Corp." Within a few weeks of setting up web pages and publishing, I had several pages in the top ten search results for Google. As of eight months later, I have nine of the top ten results.

Evocative: The title should tell the reader something about your book. For computer and math geeks, *Avogadro Corp* is an obvious play on Google's name, and, in fact, the book is set in a fictitious Google-like company. My subtitle, *The Singularity is Closer than it Appears*, clearly identifies the book as being about the technological singularity.

Pronounceable: I didn't know this ahead of time, but it turns out that it's advantageous to have a book title that can be easily pronounced and understood in person. Once you've published, it will come up in conversation quite often. I failed in this regard, as few people recognize the term Avogadro or know how to pronounce it. I've even heard it called "Avocado Corp."

However, this is the least important principle, as I easily remedied the situation by printing business cards with the book cover photo, title, and short blurb. I always have these ready, and it's even better to give people a book business card than it is to expect them to remember your title. (More on book business cards later.)

Measuring Title Effectiveness

Wouldn't it be great if, before you ever released your book, you had a way to know how catchy a title was? It is possible to do this with Google AdWords.

The approach I'm about to describe is known to work well with non-fiction books, where you have a specific target audience you want to reach, and you want your title to appeal to this audience. I'm not aware of anyone using this approach with a fiction book, but if you try it, let me know what you find.

Here's the process:

1. Brainstorm a list of potential titles.
2. From the initial list, brainstorm different ways you could order the same words to make new titles. For example, "Marketing Widgets" could also be called "How to Market Widgets", "Marketing Widgets 101", "Marketing for Widget Makers"
3. Stop when you have five to twenty titles.
4. Set up a Google AdWords account at http://adwords.google.com.
5. Set up a new advertising campaign inside AdWords. You'll want to establish a daily budget and run the

campaign for several days. How much you spend and how long you run the campaign depends on how many titles you need to test. If you are comparing five titles, a $10 daily budget run for one or two days may be enough. When I tested fourteen titles for this book, I used a $25 budget and ran for four days.

6. Under advanced campaign settings, select the option to "rotate ads indefinitely". (You don't want Google to optimize your ads. Instead, you want all of them shown equally.)

> Self-Published Author?
> Get your copy of "Indie & Small Press Book Marketing"
> williamhertling.com
>
> Self-Published Author?
> Get your copy of "Indie Marketing 101"
> williamhertling.com
>
> Self-Published Author?
> Get your copy of "Get Noticed: How to Market Your Indie Book"
> williamhertling.com

Example ads used for title testing this book.
Note how the ads are identical except for the book title.

7. Create your ads. The ads must be identical, except for the different titles you want to test. Each ad should point to a landing page that you have created for the book. This can be a draft landing page with a mailing list signup form, although the specifics aren't that important.
8. Let the ads run for the designated amount of time.
9. View the ad statistics and look at the number of clicks and the CTR (click through rate). Those ads that have more clicks and a higher CTR have a more compelling title.

This type of testing works within limits. That is, I could create an ad that read "Get free money now", and I might get a high click rate, but it doesn't truly reflect the product I'm offering the customer.

Some authors use a two-stage process. First they identify the top candidates for a title as described above. Then they repeat the test, using permutations of those candidates as title and subtitle pairs.

Ad	Labels	Status	% Served	Clicks	Impr.	CTR
Self-Published Author? Get your copy of "Indie & Small Press Book Marketing" williamhertling.com	–	Approved	6.89%	25	7,710	0.32%
Self-Published Author? Get your copy of "Indie Marketing 101" williamhertling.com	–	Approved	6.97%	16	7,801	0.21%
Self-Published Author? Get your copy of "Get Noticed: How to Market Your Indie Book" williamhertling.com	–	Approved	6.79%	15	7,600	0.20%
Self-Published Author? Get your copy of "Indie & Small Press Marketing 101" williamhertling.com	–	Approved	6.86%	15	7,677	0.20%
Self-Published Author? Get your copy of "Marketing Your Book Online" williamhertling.com	–	Approved	6.89%	13	7,707	0.17%
Self-Published Author? Get your copy of "Indie Marketing" williamhertling.com	–	Approved	6.96%	13	7,782	0.17%
Self-Published Author? Get your copy of "Viral Marketing for Books" williamhertling.com	–	Approved	6.86%	11	7,672	0.14%
Self-Published Author? Get your copy of "Viral Book Marketing" williamhertling.com	–	Approved	6.92%	11	7,746	0.14%
Self-Published Author? Get your copy of "Marketing Your Indie or Small Press Book" williamhertling.com	–	Approved	6.80%	10	7,609	0.13%
Self-Published Author? Get your copy of "Viral Marketing for Indie and Small Press Books" williamhertling.com	–	Approved	6.65%	9	7,444	0.12%
Self-Published Author? Get your copy of "How to Market Your Indie or Small Press Book" williamhertling.com	–	Approved	6.95%	9	7,777	0.12%
Self-Published Author? Get your copy of "Get Noticed: How to Market Your Book" williamhertling.com	–	Approved	6.85%	8	7,661	0.10%
Self-Published Author? Get your copy of "Get Your Book Noticed" williamhertling.com	–	Approved	6.96%	8	7,788	0.10%
Self-Published Author? Get your copy of "How to Sell 10,000 Books" williamhertling.com	–	Approved	6.93%	6	7,748	0.08%

The fourteen titles tested for this book. Notice that the top title is four times more effective than the bottom title.

Cover and Interior Design

Cover Design

The cover is one of the two most important features by which prospective readers will judge your book. A good cover will have a sense of design integrity and depth: the elements on the page will complement each other.

I created nearly a dozen covers for *Avogadro Corp* using online cover design tools at both Lulu and Createspace, two of the major print-on-demand companies. Despite my best efforts, even going so far as to order the print copies of the books, every cover I designed screamed "self-published book".

Good design doesn't have to be expensive. When I realized that I couldn't do it myself, I was fortunate to find a family member who could design a beautiful book cover. Even then, I chose to go with a simpler, less dynamic cover that looked professional, rather than attempt something fancier that I couldn't quite pull off with my available budget, skills, and friends.

In the final cover of *Avogadro Corp*, you'll notice that the font used for the title has a three-dimensional effect. The colors of the font both reflect the artwork and provide a vaguely menacing feeling. The height and weight of the font and placement of both text and artwork feels aesthetically pleasing. All of this is critically important to the final perception of the cover.

Unless you have design experience, leave this to a professional. Find a friend or family member who has design experience (preferably book cover experience), and ask them to design the cover for you, or pay a professional.

By the way, you'll see that I use photos of my own books, websites, and Amazon pages as examples throughout this text. This is because I know them very well, including all of the effort, experimentation, and decisions that went into them. There are certainly better covers and

Avogadro Corp cover design

websites out there, but I can't speak to them as personally as I can with my own experiences.

Interior design

Good interior design for a print book is also difficult. It's less of a factor in someone's purchase decision (since, in most cases, if you are indie or small press published, people will be picking up your book for the first time after they've ordered it online), but it still affects how people consider the book. A poor design that doesn't adhere to print conventions will appear amateurish and adversely affect people's perceptions. A person who would have been inspired to write a positive review on Amazon had the book been formatted perfectly, might not if the interior design detracts from reading it. Worse yet, a bad interior design might cause a person who otherwise felt neutral to write a negative review.

Just a few of the factors to be considered in interior design:

- effective choice of font family
- correct ratio of font size to page size
- correct ratio of page margins to page size
- correct interior margin considering book thickness and binding type
- page headers and footers
- chapter openings
- inter-scene formatting
- design of front and back matter
- page breaks and line breaks

Even though I am very competent when it comes to technology, have a background in printing, and a reasonable sense of design, it still took me between eighty and a hundred hours of work to research the design principles for interior layout and then perform the layout. Even then, it was close, but still not perfect. I chose to hand it off to a professional.

Example of print design evolving over time, from original manuscript on left to final design on right

Ereader Conversion

Of all the design related components, the ereader format of your book is the one piece that you can probably do yourself. I've used three different approaches to generate ereader files.

Scrivener epub and mobi export: Of all possible methods, I found this one to be the easiest, most repeatable, and most flexible. Scrivener is software for Mac and Windows computers designed specifically for writing books. One of the features that I love is the ability to organize your book by chapters and scenes, and then drag and drop the scenes to reorder them. Want to try moving a scene from one chapter to the next? It's a simple drag and drop operation. It also allows you to see the structure of your book at a glance, and skip around from scene to scene and chapter to chapter.

Scrivener has the built-in ability to export your book to the epub format, which is the format supported by most ereaders other than Amazon's Kindle. By downloading the freely available kindlegen software, Scrivener can also export to mobi, the format used by Kindle.

It takes a few minutes to set up the meta-data for your project and generate the front-matter (title page, copyright page) and back-matter (about the author, author's note). Scrivener will also generate a table of contents in the correct format, using its knowledge of the structure of your book.

If this path is available to you, I highly recommend it. Scrivener is available for both Windows and Mac from Literature and Latte (http://literatureandlatte.com/)

Microsoft Word to KDP: The second easiest approach I found was to upload a Microsoft Word document to the Kindle Direct Publishing website. If your document has simple formatting (no tables or charts, for example), it should be just an hour or two of work to get your Word document formatted correctly in order to convert to Kindle format. In some cases, generating the table of contents can be tricky.

Microsoft Word to Smashwords: Smashwords enables distribution of your ebook to a variety of ebook stores, including Apple's iTunes Bookstore, Sony's ereader bookstore, Barnes & Noble, and direct distribution via Smashwords. It's the easiest way to get into these other channels.

Unfortunately, I found the conversion process to be challenging. And even after painstaking attention to fixing the issues I encountered, my sales on Smashwords are less than one percent of my sales on Amazon, making the return-on-effort very small.

On the plus side, Smashwords is DRM-free. Some readers value this highly (to avoid getting locked into a single platform, to be able to read what they've bought anywhere they want to). So I do make my novels available on Smashwords.

If you have enough time to do everything, then use Smashwords. But if it becomes a tradeoff between getting Smashwords and all the other tasks on your launch and promotion checklist, my recommendation is to defer Smashwords until you have more time.

Web Presence and Social Media Identity

Introduction

Collectively, web presence and social media identity are the most powerful tools you'll have for promotion. Just a few of the benefits include:

- Convincing prospective readers that your book is worth buying.
- Identifying you as an author and establishing your credibility.
- Engaging with your readers.
- Amplifying the positive messages that others write about your book.
- Providing a mechanism for readers to find out about additional and future books, converting one purchase into many purchases.

To accomplish these tasks, it's necessary to prepare ahead of time. The essential tools of the trade take time to setup, learn how to use, and to build connections. I'll cover these tools one by one, but the most essential pieces are:

1. book landing page
2. blog / website

3. mailing list
4. Twitter / Facebook

Book Landing Page

Your book landing page is the go-to location to describe your book. Its primary goal is to convince visitors to buy your book.

When I started planning my promotion strategy for *Avogadro Corp*, I knew I would need a page to describe the book. I started by creating a static page on my existing blog. Then I thought of Tim Ferriss and his two New York Times best-selling books *The 4-Hour Workweek* and *The 4-Hour Body*. I knew that Tim was an expert on how to promote books: In 2011, he held a workshop on book marketing, charged $7,000 per person, and sold out every open slot.

When in doubt, do what Tim does. I visited Tim's landing page

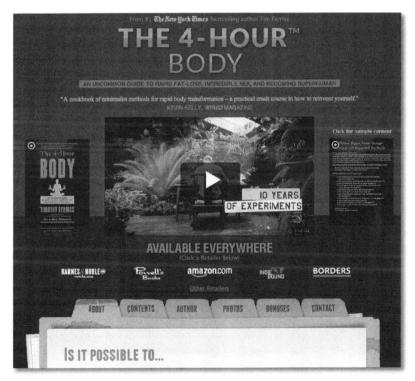

Example book landing page (fourhourbody.com)

for *The 4-Hour Body* at fourhourbody.com.

Looking at this page, here's what I notice, from top to bottom:

- Statement of credibility: "From #1 The New York Times bestselling author Tim Ferriss"
- Title and Subtitle
- Prominent, leading endorsement: "A cookbook of minimalist methods for..."
- Cover photo
- Video content
- Sample content
- Available Everywhere
- List of Retailers
- More detailed content below

The page is visually appealing and focused: it shows you a few

Avogadro Corp Landing Page at avogadrocorp.com

compelling reasons why you should purchase the book and then funnels you towards retailers.

When I considered *Avogadro Corp*, I didn't have video or sample content. But I did have an attractive cover, advance blurbs, and multiple retailers. So I used what I could of Tim Ferriss's general design, and made it my own.

Because I'm not a designer, I needed to keep the page simple. There's a focus on a clean cover image with reflection, a prominent quote at the top of the page, and available retailers. Below the "fold" (the part of the page where the reader needs to scroll down), is a list of seven blurbs from the most prominent endorsements I've received, and a small about the author section.

In summary, the key features of your book landing page:

- clean layout and design
- prominent awesome quote (even if it's just from one of your friends)
- couple of paragraphs selling the book
- snazzy, prominent book cover
- endorsements from readers -- probably sourced from amazon.com reviews.

Experimentation: A/B Testing

I did an experiment to assess the effectiveness of my landing page in January, 2011. The form of the experiment was an A/B test. Using a targeted Facebook advertisement (more on that later), I directed visitors to my landing page one week and to the Amazon.com page for Avogadro Corp the following week.

My hypothesis was that those people who were sent to the Amazon page would be more likely to buy. I thought this would be true because it would be one less click to purchase the book and because I assumed visitors would trust Amazon more than a random site on the Internet.

What I learned shocked me.

The reverse was true: People I sent to my landing page were twice as likely to purchase as people I sent directly to the Amazon page. The landing page was more effective at convincing visitors to purchase the book.

In retrospect, I believe this is because a book landing page is optimized for just one thing: putting a book forward in the best possible light to encourage the purchase. By comparison, Amazon's website is designed to encourage browsing, which means that Amazon doesn't care what product a customer buys.

Blog / Author website

The book landing page is a single web page that highlights and sells your book. But ideally you'll also have an author website that fulfills these primary goals:

1. Identify who you are as an author (e.g. "You've reached the homepage of writer John Smith, author of X, Y, and Z.")
2. Showcase the books you have for sale.
3. Have content that brings readers to your blog. For years I posted notes for every panel I went to at every conference. Gradually my traffic grew.
4. Serves as a signup location for your mailing list.

The book landing page and your author website may reside on the same or separate websites. I think the ideal is to have one website, but it's crucial to have your book landing page be as design-perfect as possible. If your blog has limitations on how much control you have over the blog, then it may be necessary to use a second website for your book landing page.

Tim Ferriss uses http://fourhourworkweek.com as his author website and the book landing page for his first book *The 4-Hour Workweek*.

As you can see, there is a small dilemma with this approach. As Tim publishes additional books, the identity of his website is mixed up with the name of his first book. For that reason, if you think there's even a small chance you'll publish multiple books, it's advantageous to use your real name as the domain name of your author website. Long before I ever considered publishing a book, I was blogging under my real name.

The example screenshot of williamhertling.com shows that it identifies who I am, hosts my blog, and showcases my books along the right hand side. There's a mailing list signup form below the fold in the navigation (or nav) bar on the right hand side.

My blog and author website at williamhertling.com

Blogging

Creating and maintaining a blog can be a wonderful way to engage in the practice of writing, engage with friends, and record important facts, events, or internet resources for your later use. Before Facebook and the slew of other social networking sites, blogs were the de facto social network of their time. And they still perform a valuable role in driving people to your website.

Some authors don't want to invest the time in blogging. They may feel that they don't have anything to say or that no one will read their blog, or they feel too shy to put themselves out in front of everyone.

I don't feel that an author must blog, but it is strongly advantageous, and in most cases easier than you think. There are two main reasons it is so helpful to authors.

The first is that it helps drive traffic to your site. The more valuable content you have on your website, the more people will find themselves there, either by finding your articles on a search engine like Google, or by finding another website that links to the articles. Each visitor to your blog is one more person who is exposed to your books, and may decide to purchase one.

The second reason is that it's a way to engage with your readers. When a reader reads and loves a book, it's tremendously rewarding to be able to visit the author's website, and discover more there.

Obviously, it's a wonderful opportunity for the reader to discover additional books by the same author, but it's also a way for the reader to build a personal connection and possibly become a dedicated fan. A dedicated fan is one who will mention an author and their books many times over in real life and online. Not only does that expose many more people to word of the author's writing, but it's also the strongest form of endorsement when a reader takes the time to tell others about a book.

Articles for blogs fall into four main categories:

1. **Original, "expert" content:** Expert content is anything in which the writer is giving their opinion or expertise. It could be an article on how to organize a kitchen, how to format a manuscript, what the author thinks of a product, a book review, etc.

2. **Curated content:** Curated content is anything in which the writer is selecting and excerpting content from somewhere else, and sharing it via their blog. It could be a link to an article on when to use commas, with a quoted paragraph, or a link to the best science fiction books as

selected by some other expert, with the top two or three books highlighted.

3. **Note-taking:** Note-taking is the simple exercise of taking notes at a conference, in a class, or of a book. It's the documentation of someone else's shared expertise.

4. **Slice of life:** Although most readers don't care what their favorite author had for lunch, in many cases they do care about certain aspects of the author's life, such as what they're reading, if they visit someplace special in the world, if they get together with another author.

The list above should demonstrate that there's a wide range of potential article topics, and that the majority of them utilize knowledge and skills you have. You may not feel like you can write the definitive treatise on genre X, but you can review books, reshare content from others, take notes at a conference, and share your life experiences. That's enough to fill any blog.

Some would-be bloggers are concerned that no one will read their blog. That's absolutely true. In the beginning, no one will read your blog. But with time, that can change.

From 2003, when I started blogging, to 2007, the only consistent readers of my blog were my mom, spouse, and a handful of friends. But in 2007, my traffic started to pick up. I was a compulsive note-taker at conferences, and I started to find that the speakers would often link to my notes of their talks. Major blogs, such as lifehacker, used my notes to compose their own articles. And some of my own, original content was reshared by others: my article How to Find the Time to Blog was one of my early popular articles. By 2011, I was getting 50,000 visitors a year to my blog.

All that traffic can help increase sales of your book. Some percentage of visitors will see that you have a book and decide to buy it. If your book and the topics you blog about are closely related, a higher percentage of visitors will convert to sales. For example, if you primarily write fantasy novels, and you blog about reviews of fantasy novels and construction of medieval armor, you'll get a good conversion of visitors into sales. On the other hand, if they are not related at all, the conversion will be low.

In my case, my visitors were coming for a wide variety of topics ranging from how-to articles on social media to customer support strategies to product reviews.

It's hard to know how many of the five thousand visitors a month converted to book sales, but if even one half of one percent bought my book, that's still twenty-five copies a month I would not have otherwise sold.

Create a blog, start writing content, and keep going. Don't blog so much that it detracts from finishing your long form writing. You still want to get that novel published. Instead, see what you can do if you invest just one hour a week in your blog.

Mailing List

After reading Tim Ferriss's *The 4-Hour Workweek*, I was so impressed by the book that I found my way to Tim's website, and started reading his blog posts about success stories and additional techniques. Once there, I saw a mailing list subscription button. Not wanting to miss any of the great content he was sharing, I subscribed to his mailing list.

In November and December, 2010, I received a few mailing list emails from Tim Ferriss about his upcoming book, *The 4-Hour Body*. Then in mid-December I received another email from Tim, this one making a personal appeal. It mentioned how he was close to breaking into *The New York Times* bestseller list. If anyone hadn't bought the book, or if anyone still needed to buy a Christmas gift for anyone, Tim asked that they consider buying copies right away.

With a flash of insight, I realized a whole bunch of things on receiving this email:

1. I still needed Christmas gifts for my mother, brother, and father.
2. Tim was a very clever marketer. (Not surprising, since this is part of what he emphasized in *The 4-Hour Workweek*.)

3. December is the best time to launch a book, because people will buy copies not just for themselves but also as gifts.
4. By having a self-selected mailing list of his most enthusiastic fans, Tim had created an army of people who were eager to help him out.
5. Unlike Facebook, Twitter, or a blog, a mailing list is the single best way to get a message out to be read by every one of the people who subscribed.

I bought three copies of *The 4-Hour Body* that same day, and I'm sure hundreds or thousands of Tim Ferriss fans did the same thing, catapulting the book to the top of the *NYT* bestseller list for that category.

Even if you choose not to blog or use Twitter or Facebook, having a mailing list is an absolute must. The reason is simple. Each person on a mailing list is both more likely to see a message from the sender and more likely to take action on it, compared to a message sent by any other mechanism. Let's compare Twitter, blogging, and an email list, with a hypothetical message sent via each of the channels asking users to buy a new book by an author. The numbers below are intended to be representative of general trends, and can of course vary.

	Twitter	Blog	Email List
Number of followers / visitors / subscribers	100,000	100,000	100,000
Number who will see a given message	5,000 (5%)	10,000 (10%)	50,000 (50%)
Number of above who will take action	50 (1%)	300 (3%)	5,000 (10%)

In the Twitter case, when a user with 100,000 followers posts a message, only a very small number of his or her followers will see the message (5%). That's because Twitter is a "dip a toe in the stream" sort of service, rather than a queue of messages where the goal is to read them all. (Many users follow many hundreds of other users, and thousands of messages stream by each day.) Of those who do see the example message, because Twitter is largely a surfing activity (rather than a doing activity) and because the size of the message prohibits crafting a compelling call to action, only a small percentage do something (1%), e.g. Fifty people buy a book.

In the blog case, a blog with a 100,000 monthly visitors may still only have a relatively small number who see a given post (10%), because visitors may be coming via search engines to see older posts, or because the occasional visitor may read some but not all posts. In this format, because a more compelling case to take action can be crafted using more words and photos, we assume triple the number who see the message will take action. This would result in selling 300 books.

Finally, in the email case, we know that most people read their email. From the data that's available in the mailing list service I use, I know that fifty to sixty percent of my subscribers typically open an email, and that's representative of most mailing lists. Finally, because these are people who have self-selected to be on the mailing lists, and because people who are reading email tend to be in more of a doing, rather than surfing mindset, we can assume about ten percent will take action. This would result in a whopping 5,000 books sold.

In the real world, few people have a hundred thousand people on a mailing list. In fact, it's generally easier to get Twitter followers or blog readers. But hopefully the example indicates that email subscribers are an author's best friends: they are your most loyal fans, the people who are as eager to help you find success as you are.

Fortunately, it's easy to create a mailing list using a web service. I use Mail Chimp (http://mailchimp.com) to create and manage my own mailing list.

There are two different approaches to creating the content to send to a mailing list. In one case, all blog posts are automatically emailed out to all subscribers. In the alternative case, you compose periodic emails specifically for the mailing list subscribers. You can choose from either approach. Tim Ferriss's blog posts are all high-quality, expert content, so it makes sense that subscribers would like to receive all of his posts. By comparison, my blog posts are a mish-mash of curated content, conference notes, and expert content. Because I don't want to inundate my subscribers with too much raw material, I choose to explicitly write a monthly subscriber email.

I'll provide example emails in Phase 3, but a typical monthly update email might include:

- What I'm up to this month (writing, editing, etc.)
- Noteworthy accomplishments or accolades for my books (winning awards, endorsements from influencers, hitting a high point on a bestseller list)
- Mini-reviews and endorsements of especially good books I've read.
- A call to action (write a review, tell a friend, buy the next book, etc.)

Social Networks

Social networking and microblogging services like Facebook, Twitter, Google Plus, and LinkedIn are a valuable way to connect with readers, stay in touch with trends, follow fellow authors, make announcements, and direct traffic to your blog.

I participate in all four services, although I use each one differently. On a day to day basis, I use Facebook the most, both because it's convenient and because it's where I'm engaging with my friends anyway. However, I also make a point of using Twitter at least weekly.

I think you should participate in at least one of Facebook or Twitter, if not both.

I'll discuss how to make the most use of these services in later sections of the book. For now, consider that you'll want to be actively using these services for anywhere from one to four hours a week to become familiar with them and build relationships.

The super secret tip: Think of these as professional networking tools. The goal as a writer is not to share photos of cats, your kids, or your meals. It's to engage in whatever kinds of communities you would be involved with in the real world. Do you write science fiction? Network with scientists and other science fiction writers.

It's important to become a user of these services before your book is published. You can't show up to Twitter on the day you publish and expect to understand what's happening or how to make a big splash.

Call to Action

The last thing to you need to consider about book promotion before you publish is the inclusion of an appeal to the reader in the after-matter of your book. While a reader is still basking in the glow of your amazing ending is the best possible time to get them to write a review, buy the next book in the series, or sign up for your mailing list so they can find out when your next book is released. This is the <u>call to action</u>.

Here's how: Immediately after the end of the story, make an appeal to the reader: "If you liked this book, won't you please tell a friend or post a review?" Link to the Amazon review page in the digital version. Also direct people to your blog: "Sign up for my mailing list so you can find out when my next book is released."

I didn't figure this out until I released my second book. I had very few mailing list signups when I first published *Avogadro Corp*. Now I see them trickling in every day.

Other content to potentially include in the book itself:

- A link to your website near the front of the book.
- Your email address if you'd like to hear from fans.

Dear Reader,

Thanks for buying Avogadro Corp: The Singularity Is Closer Than It Appears. I hope you enjoyed it.

As an independent author, I don't have a marketing department or the exposure of being on bookshelves. If you enjoyed Avogadro Corp, please help spread the word and support the writing of the rest of the series by writing an Amazon review or telling a few friends about the book.

- Write a review on Amazon.

- Buy the next book in the series: A.I. Apocalypse.

- Subscribe to my monthly newsletter at williamhertling.com if you'd like to find out when the final book in the series, The Last Firewall, is released.

Thanks again,

William Hertling

P.S. Keep reading for a free preview of the next book in the series, A.I. Apocalypse.

Example after-matter appeal to the reader

Business Cards

Business cards are surprisingly handy for books. They can:
- turn a chance encounter with a stranger into an opportunity for them to purchase your book
- increase the likelihood of a friend buying
- overcome shortcomings in your author name or your title (e.g. hard to remember or spell, very common, etc.)
- make the case for purchase by including praise, blurbs, and a cover photo
- connect you to a reviewer or reader by including your contact information

- advertise your book at your local supermarkets or coffee shops, which often have bulletin boards for business cards
- serve as ad-hoc advertising at a conference (leave them on tables)

I used VistaPrint to create cards. It's surprisingly inexpensive (about $30 for 500 cards). If you need them for an event, order well ahead of time so that you don't have to pay for express manufacturing or shipping, which can dwarf the cost of the cards themselves.

Avogadro Corp
The Singularity Is Closer Than It Appears

Avogadro Corp is about the creation and subsequent race to contain an artificial intelligence as it begins to gain power, hiring and firing employees, transferring corporate funds, and arming itself.

http://avogadrocorp.com

William Hertling
http://www.williamhertling.com

Example business card front with title, pitch, author, and url.

Praise for Singularity Series

"A tremendous book everyone must read." — BRAD FELD, cofounder TechStars

"Highly entertaining, gripping, and thought inspiring. Don't start without the time to finish." — GIFFORD PINCHOT III, author THE INTELLIGENT ORGANIZATION.

"A fascinating look at how simple and benign advancements in technology could lead to the surprise arrival of the first AI. Like all good techno-thrillers, the reality of AI is less than ideal." —JASON GLASPEY of SILICON FLORIST

"I found myself reading with a sense of awe, and read it way too late into the night." — GENE KIM, author VISIBLE OPS

Author Contact: William Hertling

Example business card back with praise and
author contact info at bottom (not shown)

Phase 1 Checklist

- ☐ Book Focused
  - ☐ Get feedback and make improvements
  - ☐ Get copy-editing help
  - ☐ Get proof-reading help
  - ☐ Choose title
  - ☐ Run title effectiveness testing
  - ☐ Get professional cover design
  - ☐ Interior design
  - ☐ Ereader conversion
  - ☐ Include after-matter call to action
- ☐ Web/Social Media
  - ☐ Create book landing page
  - ☐ Establish blog
  - ☐ Write at least five blog posts
  - ☐ Create mailing list
  - ☐ Sign up and use Facebook and Twitter
- ☐ Create and order business cards

Phase 2: Book Launch

Goals

These are the goals of your initial book launch, which I'll define as the first month of sales:

- Drive enough sales to get into Amazon's recommendation engine
- Gain at least twenty reviews, establishing a minimum level of credibility
- Get mentions on web and social media sites

Timing

If you can time the release of your book to December, this is ideal. Not only can you take advantage of the fact that this is the highest book buying month, but you can specifically appeal to friends and family to buy a copy not just for themselves, but as gifts for other people. My closest friends bought two, three, or even five copies.

If you cannot launch in November or December to take advantage of the holiday buying season, then your next best bets are either January through April or October.

Avoid May through August. Starting in May, book buying decreases, and sales are notoriously slow during the summer. The only exception to this is academic and educational texts, which could be launched in the summer for back-to-school sales.

Simultaneous Kindle/Print

When a person visits an Amazon product page, the first impression is dominated by just five pieces of information: the book title, cover, reviews, price, and available formats. Therefore, as an author, it makes sense to make each of these five as compelling as possible, and that includes the available formats in which a book is available. In particular, the formats box is one of the largest elements on the page, comparable only to the cover, so it has significant visual impact.

As authors, we work really hard to make sure the title and cover are the best they can be. So what can we do for the formats?

I've personally noticed that when I look through books on Amazon, I tend to feel more confident about buying books that are available in more formats. They feel more professional, less fly-by-night. They give the impression of a successful book.

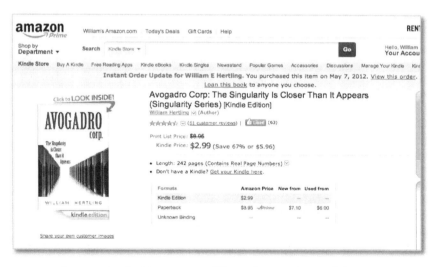

Amazon product page: cover, title, reviews, price, and formats

The most basic step to take is to ensure that both Kindle and print versions are available and linked together before you starting telling people about your book. Having two formats builds credibility. It also ensures that when you make an appeal to friends and family (described next), you're maximizing the impact of that appeal because you are supporting the most commonly purchased formats.

Week by Week Schedule

Week 0: Publish

When I published *Avogadro Corp*, I had no idea how long it would take to publish once I had the final digital files. After all, it's so exciting to finally see my book available that each hour I had to wait seemed like an eternity.

I used Amazon's Kindle Direct Publishing (KDP) website to publish the Kindle version of my book. I strongly recommend this approach. The tools available for Kindle publishing are great, whether you use KDP's ability to convert a Microsoft Word .doc file, or directly upload a .mobi file generated by Scrivener or another tool. I used both: *Avogadro Corp* was done with the Word converter, and *A.I. Apocalypse* with Scrivener mobi generation.

I used Amazon's Createspace, a print-on-demand (POD) service, for the paperback version of *Avogadro Corp*. Print-on-demand books have the same high quality as other trade paperback books you've read, and Createspace manufactures them so quickly (in just a few hours), that a buyer will receive them as quickly as if they ordered a pre-manufactured book. Print-on-demand allows the publisher to avoid the upfront cost of a large print run and the hassle of managing inventory. There is a slight cost disadvantage, although it's not much, and I think the benefits of POD outweigh the disadvantages.

The Kindle version of your book will take 24 to 48 hours from the time you press the button in the Kindle Direct Publishing (KDP) website until the book is available in Amazon. The print version takes much longer. First the files are uploaded, then a proof copy is printed and mailed to you. After you approve it, it will still take two to three days before the book is available online. Finally, one both books are available, it takes a day or so before the two formats are linked together on the Amazon website. This might not seem like much time, but if you're carefully orchestrating a December launch, like I did for *Avogadro Corp*, it eats away at the precious days before Christmas.

For the indie published:

If you absolutely cannot convert your book into the Kindle format yourself, you'll need to hire someone to do it. The person or company you hire should be able to provide samples of books they've previously converted to Kindle format. Check these to make sure the formatting is good, that they contain a table of contents, that the font size is appropriate and can be scaled using the font size feature of the Kindle. If you don't have a Kindle, you can do this with Kindle software on your computer, although this is a good excuse to buy a Kindle.

Also, inquire ahead of time how much it costs to handle corrections to the Kindle format of your book. One of the benefits of ereaders is that it's easy to handle corrections to the text. *Avogadro Corp* has had three revisions over eight months.

At the current point in time, I don't recommend Createspace's Kindle conversion service. I've seen one Createspace generated Kindle book in which the main font was half the size it should be, forcing me to maximize the Kindle font just to bring it back to a normal size.

There's an intrinsic difference between what is uploaded to KDP and Createspace. Ereaders need flowing content, like a Word file or mobi file. By comparison, the ideal file for Createspace is a PDF file, in which text does not flow from page to page. (The text appears to flow, but behind the scenes, it's laid out in a static, non-flowing format.) For this reason, as of 2012, I'd be somewhat suspect of services that claim to generate Kindle files from PDFs. I think it's too risky that the conversion would have errors in it.

Unless you are a designer yourself, I assume you will use a professional to generate the print-ready PDF files yourself for Createspace. It's a relatively simple process to upload the files.

It is possible to use Microsoft Word or an equivalent to generate print ready files, but please take the time to ensure your book looks and feels professional, as discussed in Phase 1.

For the small press published:

Your publisher will take care of generating the necessary files and uploading them to Amazon. Congratulations! This will relieve a burden from you.

I recommend that you discuss with your publisher how frequently and with what granularity will they report sales data to you. For the third phase of book marketing, it becomes important to have timely access to sales data, ideally on a day-by-day basis. If you are testing versions of an advertisement, landing page, email campaign, website design, or text on your Amazon page, you'll need some way to see the effect on sales. With day by day reporting, you can see the effects of changes within a few days. With week-by-week reporting, it could take several weeks to run even a simple experiment comparing one variable. With monthly reporting, it would take months to test just one component.

If your publisher is hesitant to provide data more frequently and with daily granularity, be sure to explain that you want to use the data to optimize your own marketing. While they might not appreciate having to pull and report the data more frequently, they will appreciate an author who is highly involved in their own marketing.

Amazon Author Central

Have you ever wondered where the Editorial Reviews section of an Amazon page comes from, or why some authors have an Amazon author page with a headshot, bio, and book listing? These are thanks to Amazon Author Central. You can access it at http://authorcentral.amazon.com.

In addition to setting up your biography statement, headshot, and RSS feed for your blog, you can also edit additional information about each book, create author events, and link to your Twitter feed.

Additional sales data, your author sales rank, and a consolidated view of customer reviews are all available through Author Central.

Amazon Author Central: Set up your author profile, claim your books and edit their extended information

Week 1: Close Friends and Family Appeal

Once your books are available for sale on Amazon and linked together, it's time to make the first appeal to friends and family.

I started with an email to my closest friends, about 15 people. You can use anywhere from 10 to 25 people. I chose a small enough group that it would be intimate (most of the people know each other, or at least of each other). I knew I could follow up with them several times, and they wouldn't mind. And because of the small size, they would know that their individual actions mattered. And finally, most especially, I was looking for people who would be making a purchase based on my personal appeal and not the merits of the book. After all, with zero reviews, a new book doesn't have much credibility based on its own.

Most of my closest friends already knew that this was a book I'd been working on for close to two years. If they didn't, I'd be sure to mention it. As you can see from the email, it emphasizes the two critical actions needed: for them to buy the book and post a review. It might not hurt to mention the goals either (getting twenty reviews and

---

Hi friends,

For those of you that haven't heard, my first novel, *Avogadro Corp*, is up on Amazon now. If you haven't seen it yet, you can check it out at: http://amzn.to/avogadrocorp

There's two things that help get a book noticed on Amazon: sales and reviews. Both sales and reviews generate recommendations, help your book show up in search results, increase the number of people that click on a book, and ultimately generate sales.

If you've already bought a copy - THANK YOU! It means so much to me.

You can buy a copy for yourself or give a copy as a gift to a friend (you can give a Kindle copy to anyone with a Kindle, iPad, or iPhone - just click Give as a Gift, and then provide their email address.)

And if you've read *Avogadro Corp* and enjoyed it, a positive review would be a tremendous help! It doesn't have to be long - a short rating is still powerful! You click "Create Your Own Review" in the reviews area, select a star rating, and enter a short title and a few sentences. That's it!

Again, here's the link to *Avogadro Corp*:

http://amzn.to/avogadrocorp

Thank you for all your help during the creative process - your encouragement, feedback, writing critique, editing, proofreading, and design. I couldn't have done it without you!

Thanks,

Will

Example email sent to friends and family

fifty sales), although I didn't think to do so in my original email.

After a few days, I checked my sales statistics, and found out how many books I sold. I sent another email mid-week telling them how many copies I sold, sharing with them my excitement, thanking them for their support, and reminding them to buy a copy if they hadn't already.

After a week, I followed up again, this time mentioning how many reviews I had, how many I needed, thanking them, and asking again for them to post a review if they hadn't.

Wow -- what an amazing week it's been! I just wanted to say thank you for all the incredible well-wishes, feedback, and support with my book.

In just four short days, Avogadro has received eight great Amazon reviews, briefly got into the top 50 bestselling technothrillers, and I've received so many wonderful emails from everyone. It's been really nice.

I really don't want to spam my friends and family, so if you're interested in any further updates about Avogadro Corp or my future books just reply back with a "yes" or an email address, and I'll add you to a special email list for people who want updates.

In the meantime, a few other tidbits:

1) If you read and enjoyed it, an Amazon review is a tremendous help to promote more sales. Just a sentence or two and your star rating will make a difference.

2) In case you're wondering, it is possible to buy a Kindle version as a gift. This has been a frequent question. On the Kindle page for the book (http://amzn.to/avogadrocorp) just click the "Give as gift" button on the right side. You just need the recipient's email address.

Love and thanks and happy holidays,

Will

Example follow-up email to friends and family

As a final step, I followed up by phone or email individually to let people know how important this was for me. If you suspect cost might be an issue for someone, but think they'll post a review if they read it, offer to buy them a copy.

Most importantly, remember that this is a personal appeal based on your relationship. Your parents and close friends may not be fans of deep space science fiction or vampire urban fantasy, but they are fans of you. Emphasize the journey you've taken to get published and the excitement you feel at finally being published.

Week 2: Wide-spread Appeal

Once you have three to five reviews posted to establish a minimum level of credibility, it's time for a broader email.

I searched through my inbox to find everyone I'd emailed within the last year or two. (If you use Gmail, you can use Gmail Email Address Extractor to do this: https://gmailextract.com/)

Compose an email. In it, talk about the excitement of publishing. Sell both the book and the excitement of your journey. Just as you did in the first email, ask people to buy and then to review your book.

Five to seven days after sending this initial email, send a follow up email. Tell people about the results. Ask them to buy if they haven't, and thank the people who have. Give them all the credit.

In this follow-up email, which should be your second email to the group, tell them that you don't want to spam them unnecessarily. Ask them to reply back to you if they'd like to get future email updates. Explain you won't email more than once a month. Many people will reply yes. This is the seed of your ongoing mailing list.

Here's the follow-up email I sent out a week later:

You may have heard the exciting news, but if not, here it is: After a two year journey, my novel Avogadro Corp: The Singularity Is Closer Than It Appears is published!

Avogadro Corp is a techno-thriller about the accidental creation of an artificial intelligence at the world's largest Internet company, and the subsequent race to contain the AI, as it starts to manipulate people, transfer funds, and arm itself.

Set largely in Portland, Oregon, Avogadro Corp started as the result of a challenge to describe a realistic scenario for a human-level artificial intelligence to emerge. Here are some of the early quotes:

"Hertling builds a picture of how an AI could emerge, piece by piece, from technology available today. A fascinating and utterly believable scenario - I hope nobody tries this at home."

"An alarming and jaw-dropping tale about how something as innocuous as email can subvert an entire organization."

It's available in paperback, for the kindle, and in epub format for a variety of other ereaders.

If you've already bought a copy - THANK YOU! It means so much to me.

If not, I hope you'll buy a copy and enjoy it, or consider giving it as a gift to someone who loves techno-thrillers or science fiction.

Writing Avogadro Corp was incredibly fun, and the path to publication was a great learning experience. But now that it's published, the next challenge I face is to help it rise above the noise of thousands of other books.

Here's just a few of the things that help a book get noticed: sharing it on Facebook or Twitter, buying it or giving it as a gift, providing a review on Amazon, blog posts that link to it, emails to friends about it.

Anything you can do to help support my book would be tremendous!

Example of the broader email I sent for Avogadro Corp

I also sent a very similar email to a select few people at my work. Many employers have policies that prohibit employees from soliciting fellow employees. I would suggest that you follow your company's policy, and, in any case, stick to only those coworkers with whom you have a relationship above and beyond the ordinary coworker relationship.

Mailing List

As I previously mentioned, I use MailChimp to manage my mailing list. I started with about fifty people who said they wanted to be on it in response to my follow up email, and it's grown organically to several hundred people. MailChimp is free for the level of usage most authors would need. Here's a link to use the service: http://eepurl.com/nDMfl

You can integrate MailChimp into your website. I'll talk more about what to do with it in the next section. For now, take people who want to be on your mailing list, and manually add their email addresses to your MailChimp list.

Asking for Reviews and Acting on Feedback

Most people believe that posting fake reviews and paying for reviews are ethically wrong. Certainly, it is against Amazon's policies and may get you banned from Amazon and other bookstores. I also think it's wrong to ask friends to post falsely-positive reviews.

Some people even feel that asking for reviews may be inappropriate. I disagree. Many businesses, including retail stores, professionals, and doctors will all say something like "If you like our service/product, please tell a friend". Asking for an unbiased review is no different.

To stay clear of any ethical dilemmas, don't ask people to post only positive reviews or to be rated highly. Simply tell them how important it is to have reviews. If you've written a quality book, people will give you positive reviews. If you've written a poor book, your friends will generally not post reviews, and strangers may post negative reviews.

If you're in the situation where some of the first reviews you get are negative, or you're asking friends and family for reviews and no one will review it, you may want to take a step back and see if you're getting a sign that there are weaknesses in the book you've published.

If so, this would be the best time to fix them. If you've heard complaints about spelling or grammar errors, it's not too late to hire a proofreader or editor to fix them. If the issues are deeper (e.g. the story structure or plot is weak), you may need some expert advice: a writing class, a critique group, etc. Mistakes can be fixed, and it's better to do so before you have many negative reviews.

Week 3: Influencers and Social Network

Some people, known as influencers, have a large network of contacts and large effect on the world around them. Influencers can be bloggers, Twitter users with a large number of followers, newspaper reporters, experts in a field, a head of a company, or simply someone with a large network of friends.

If you know any influencers personally, you should go out of your way to let them know about your book. Buy them a copy and let them know you're sending them a free review copy. If I know them online, I usually buy them a Kindle copy, with an offer to send them a paperback if they'd prefer it. For people you can personally meet, bring them a physical copy. It's important to sell them not just on the book, but also on the excitement of the journey, on what you learned along the way, or the topics covered in the book.

No one is too big or small to approach. If someone has a blog and a hundred people read it each month, that's great. If you know someone with a million followers, that's awesome. (They may get pestered with requests, but it shouldn't hold you back from asking. I'll talk more in the last section about the favor economy, and what you can do to maximize your success landing the big fish.)

In my case, I bought Kindle copies for about half a dozen people. One of them posted a mention on Twitter. But another, Jason Glaspey, a local Portland entrepreneur in the tech startup scene, posted a review on Silicon Florist, a tech blog covering the startup scene in Portland. Silicon Florist has about two thousand readers, and the post helped sell between eighty and one hundred copies over the course of two weeks.

It's also time to use your social network to build sales. Now that your book has some basic credibility in the form of an Amazon sales rank and some reviews, you can use Twitter, Facebook, LinkedIn, and Google Plus to share the news of your publication. Aside from a straightforward announcement of publication, you can do additional posts that highlight positive reviews you've received, particularly good sales days, or anything else noteworthy.

It's also time to update your book landing page. Even though you probably spent weeks carefully crafting the pitch for your book, you'll find that readers usually come up with unique ways to describe your book that are better than anything you thought of. Quote single lines from reviews and include them as blurbs on the landing page. It's ideal if you obtain permission from the reviewer (which is easier in the early days because many reviews will be from friends or friends of friends that you can contact), although it's generally acceptable to quote a line from any public review (e.g. Amazon review or blog post). Here are some examples from *Avogadro Corp*:

- "A highly entertaining, gripping, thought inspiring book. Don't start without the time to finish -- it won't let you go." -- Gifford Pinchot III, founder Bainbridge Graduate Institute, author *The Intelligent Organization*.
- "An alarming and jaw-dropping tale about how something as innocuous as email can subvert an entire organization. I found myself reading with a sense of awe, and read it way too late into the night." -- Gene Kim, author *Visible Ops*
- "*Avogadro Corp* is a fascinating look at how simple and benign advancements in technology could lead to the surprise arrival of the first AI. And like all good techno-thrillers, the reality of AI is less than ideal." -- Jason Glaspey, founder paleoplan.com, bacn.com, unthirsty.com

- "HAL, the self aware CPU from 2001 a Space Odyssey is a kitten compared to ELOPe." -- Shawn Chesser, author *Trudge* and *Soldier On*
- "A fictional world where Portland is the hub for the most exciting advancements in technology... jam packed with great references to deep Portland culture." -- *Silicon Florist*

You can use these some of these same blurbs in the Amazon description, on business cards, on your blog, or anywhere you want people to be excited about your book. Blurbs have added credibility because they come from third parties and usually generate excitement because they come from a unique voice -- someone who read the book as a reader, not as the author.

Week 4: Launch Party

It's time to hold a book launch party. In reality, this could happen at any point after publication, but I think it's advantageous to do after the book has been out for a few weeks.

There are multiple purposes to the party:

- It's a celebration for you, the author, on a major accomplishment. Publication is the biggest milestone an author has, and it's worth celebrating with a party.
- It's a thank you party for your friends who have supported you by reading what you've written, buying your book, and telling their friends about it.
- It's a final kick in the pants to your friends who have been on the wall about whether they'd buy your book or not. Hopefully this will push them over the edge.

For *Avogadro Corp*, I had a party in my house. I bought alcohol and food. (It was my biggest single expense in publishing *Avogadro Corp*.) If you launch in December, you can call it a combination holiday/book launch party, if that makes you feel more comfortable.

There's two ways to get a paperback book into someone's hand. The first is that they can buy the book themselves on Amazon. The second is that you, as the author, can order books at a discount through Createspace (or your publisher in the case of small press publication). In fact, you'll probably earn more money by ordering the books at a discount, then selling them directly to friends. But don't do it! Here's why:

I had only a modest number of paperback books on hand. I told people in the invitation that I only had a few books, and that if they wanted me to sign a book, I strongly preferred if they bought the book at Amazon and brought it with them. In part, I did this because I didn't want to lay out the cash to order too many books. But the main reason I did it this way is because of Amazon's recommendation engine. When enough customers buy your book from Amazon, it will start showing up in the Amazon recommendation engine. For example, if you go today to Daniel Suarez's Amazon page for his recent technothriller, *Kill Decision*, you'll find *Avogadro Corp* listed in the recommendation area.

Over time, the recommendation engine on Amazon will likely be one of the main contributors to your sales. So I strongly prefer people buy books through Amazon, which increases the number of times that my books will appear in those recommendation areas.

Although it's possible, in theory, to hold the party the day your books are published, in practice this is tricky. You can't be sure what hiccups may delay your launch (a last minute typo fix, a cover that doesn't print well, a delay in Amazon's publication engine). And it

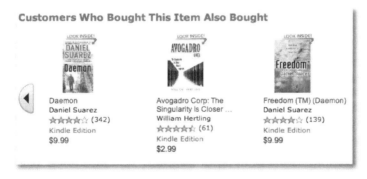

The recommendation section of Daniel Suarez's Kill Decision book on Amazon

---

Things That Can Help Promote *Avogadro Corp*

Want to help?

More than a million new books are published each year. The biggest challenge for any new author is to get his or her book noticed. There are a slew of actions that can help. Some, like sharing on Facebook and posting a review on Amazon are easy and have a big impact.

Please take a copy of this sheet if you're be able to help.

Five minutes or less:
- Post a review on Amazon. (Even two or three sentences helps.)
- Share on Facebook, Google Plus, or Twitter.
- Sign up for my mailing list at http://www.williamhertling.com.
- Tell a couple of friends about it the old-fashioned way.

Five to Fifteen Minutes:
- Post a review on Goodreads or Shelfari.
- Add to lists on Goodreads or Shelfari. Example lists might include: cyberpunk, technothriller, scifi, computers, artificial intelligence.
- Post a review or a link on your blog.
- Know any big-time bloggers or reporters? An email introduction would be awesome, so I could send them a review copy.

Other random ideas:
- I'm happy to talk to groups about A.I., computer security or privacy, or the state of the publishing industry.
- If you have ideas of what I can do, let me know!

Thanks,
Will

Index cards I distributed at my launch party

won't be possible for your guests to order the book themselves, online, before the party.

Invite everyone you know to your book launch party. I invited my kid's classmates' parents that I'd never met before. It's all good. Sell books, sign books, thank people, and have fun.

But wait! There's one more thing. I made small index cards and gave them to everyone who came to the party. The cards had a list of ten things people could do to help promote sales of my book.

Conceptual Framework

The concept behind the schedule presented is to start by marketing your book to the people with which you have the most personal credibility and deepest relationship. Initial sales and relationships will help build the credibility around your book, which then allows you to reach successively broader audiences.

You can follow this conceptual model even if you don't have the exact groups described. If, for whatever reason, you don't have very close friends and family you can rely on, substitute whatever group of people you are closest with, and understand that you may need to adapt your appeal to the group. Those closest to you will respond most to a personal argument, while those farthest from you will respond based on the merits of the book.

Accomplishments

Keep track of your accomplishments. By making a habit of keeping track of what works and doesn't work, over time you'll learn what works best for you, your genre, and your book.

As a sense of calibration, by the end of my first month of sales, I had:

- 238 books sold
- 21 reviews
- A review on one moderately prominent blog (~2,000 readers)
- A few dozen social media mentions

Phase 2 Checklist

- [ ] Time for November/December launch if possible, otherwise January to April.
- [ ] Simultaneous launch of Kindle/Print formats
- [ ] Week 0 date: _____
  - [ ] Publish
  - [ ] Kindle (allow 48 hours)
  - [ ] Print (allow 1 week)
  - [ ] Ensure print and kindle pages are linked on Amazon
  - [ ] Set up opt-in mailing list (e.g. MailChimp)
  - [ ] Set up Author Central profile and book descriptions
- [ ] Week 1 date: _____
  - [ ] Close friends and family appeal
  - [ ] Learn how to check sales reports
  - [ ] Make follow-up appeal
- [ ] Week 2 date: _____
  - [ ] Wide-spread friends, family, coworker appeal
  - [ ] Follow-up appeal with solicitation to join mailing list
- [ ] Week 3 date: _____
  - [ ] Send review copies to influencers
  - [ ] Update landing page with testimonials from reviews
  - [ ] Use social media to share news, including good reviews, sales milestones, etc.
- [ ] Week 4 date: _____
  - [ ] Hold book launch party

Phase 3: Post-Launch

Overview

In the third phase of book marketing, it's time to switch gears. You've hopefully kicked things off with a great launch giving you reviews and blurbs to build credibility and initial sales to seed the Amazon recommendation engine.

In this phase, you'll switch gears and conduct advertising experiments and intensively monitor social media, blog traffic, and web mentions to amplify mentions and expand presence.

Goals

- Amplify social media mentions
- Expand presence
- Follow up with fans, especially any influencers
- Conduct targeted advertising experiments

Mentions and Inbound Links

I search at least once a week for mentions of my book and my name, and analyze the inbound links to my blog. By doing this, I can discover:

- reviews on blogs
- mentions on Twitter
- recommendation engines that have picked up the book

I do this because I want to amplify and build connections. If someone tweets about the book with a cool quote, I want to retweet it. If someone blogs about it, I might want to comment on their blog or link to it from my Facebook page.

I may also want to build a personal connection. I could do that with a simple reply on Twitter, comment on a blog, or go a step further and email them.

Here are the tools I use.

On the web: Use Google's ability to filter searches to those within the last 24 hours or 7 days. Start by entering a search term in the search box, then select Show search tools in the left hand column. Then choose Past 24 hours or Past week.

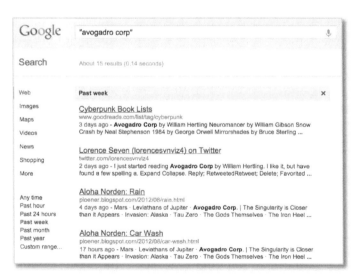

Date restricted Google Search for Avogadro Corp

For Twitter: Use a tool like TweetDeck or Hootsuite that let you set up search terms that appear as columns. You can instantly see when anyone posts something contain those terms.

TweetDeck search for "Avogadro Corp" shows most recent mentions

Inbound links: It's ideal to know how people are getting to your blog and landing page. The technical term is "referrer", although it

StatCounter "Recent Came From" shows where most recent visitors came from

may also be listed as came from, inbound links or referrals. Some blog sites have built in tools to see referrers, or you can use a tracking tool like StatCounter or Google Analytics to see who is sending visitors to your blog. Setting up tools like StatCounter require some technical expertise, and you may need help from a friend or a professional if you're not comfortable doing it yourself.

Google Alerts: Make it easy on yourself by setting up Google Alerts on your name and book title. Google will then email you when new search results appear in their database that match the search terms you are interested in. To get started, go to http://www.google.com/alerts. Put your name or title or other search into the Search query box, then select the frequency you would prefer: as it happens, daily, or weekly. (I use weekly.)

Reviews: Check the Amazon product page for your book to see recent reviews. Reviews are listed in reverse chronological order (most recent first) on the right-hand side of the page in the review section. Alternatively, you can click through to the review page, and then

Most Recent Customer Reviews

★★★★★ **Better than the first book!**
I don't do many reviews, but felt I should for this book.
I read the first book in this series, and found it to be pretty good, but seemed a little rushed or slightly thin in... Read more
Published 3 days ago by Jerome O. Pinkney

★★★★★ **I thought this was great!**
I reviewed the first book in this series and thought it was excellent.

This story is a while further into the future and for a moment, at an incident with a drone and... Read more
Published 4 days ago by John Wilkinson

★★★★☆ **Really good AI scifi, a really good read.**
This is the second book in what is shaping up to be a really good series. The AI that came to life in the first novel in the series is joined by more artificial life and then the... Read more
Published 8 days ago by Michael Poore

Most recent reviews (appears on right hand side of book page)

choose how to sort all of the reviews.

Hopefully the vast majority of reviews are positive. And indeed, people who really like a book do seem to be more likely to be invested enough to leave a review than people who only feel lukewarm about a book. On the flip side, people who really dislike a book will leave one-star reviews. However, use each review as a learning opportunity. As I mentioned before, if your novel suffers from spelling errors, grammar mistakes, or formatting issues, these are fixable problems. You may need to hire a professional to help, but don't let these issues get you down or stand between you and success. Fix them!

Other issues can be more challenging to fix. My first novel suffered from flat characters, a few of which are little more than cardboard cutouts. It turns out that, for many fans, this is not a barrier to enjoying the book. Readers who focus mostly on the plot and big ideas, like the implications for the future and technology, love the book. It's not possible to please everyone. That said, as I wrote my second and third novels, I have pushed myself to breathe more life into my characters.

Follow up with Fans

So using Google Search and Twitter you've found fans of your novel. Or perhaps they've found you, and sent you an email or direct message. What do you do?

It's important to do something. They've given you a gift by reading, enjoying, and sharing their enjoyment of the book. Now it's time to give them something in return.

- Depending on what a reader says, I might reach out to them and share some of my own enthusiasm for the book. I can tell them the story of how I came to write the book.
- I can thank them.
- I can ask them what they enjoyed.
- If they contacted me via a social media profile (or link to one in their email), I can learn a little about them, and maybe guess at why they liked the book, e.g. "I see that

you're a technology strategist. What did you think about the technology in the book?"

- If they have an interesting social media profile, you can follow them.

It can be both rewarding and insightful, so enjoy these conversations and use them as opportunities to see how other people perceive your writing and appreciate your work.

Your biggest fans may mention your book dozens of times or more to other people, online and off, potentially expanding your reach hundreds of times more than you could achieve on your own.

Connect with Communities

Connecting with communities is about discovering and engaging with those communities of people who will have a natural interest in your book, and with which you are able to engage.

Some books immediately resonate with a particular crowd of people. For example, Cory Doctorow's books, written by a software geek and frequently featuring software programmer characters, are well loved by many programmers. Dan Brown's *The Da Vinci Code* spread virally among conspiracy theorists and symbologists.

Conversely, certain groups will be opposed to certain types of books. An online group dedicated to space-faring science fiction isn't likely to take an interest (as a group) in vampire urban fantasy.

Some communities of people are defined by their interest in a genre of writing. For example, io9 is a popular science fiction blog where the authors of articles and readers of the blog are interested in science fiction. SFFWorld.com hosts discussion forums to discuss science fiction. These might seem to be attraction to an author of that genre, but there are others kinds of communities that may be more accessible.

Some groups are defined by being interested in a real-world topic. For example, there are groups of people online who are interested in autistic children, the future, living off the grid, or sailing.

If you've written a romance novel about sailing, it may be attractive to people who read romance novels, and it may be attractive to people who have an interest in sailing. Both are viable communities to try to connect with.

But you may find it easier to connect with the sailing community than with a community around romance novels. There are many thousands of romance novels published, and any community that exists will likely be inundated with "read my romance novel" messages. By comparison, the sailing community is much more specific, and a sailing romance novel might be fairly unique, so the community may be more receptive to such a novel.

It's not always obvious what communities will have an interest in a book. When I published *Avogadro Corp*, I thought my novel would appeal to three groups:

- Readers of science fiction: a big group, and yet one that's hard to reach as a whole.
- Fans of Charles Stross and Cory Doctorow: these are authors whom I admire and whom deal with somewhat similar topics.
- People interested in the technological singularity: The singularity is the point at which artificial intelligence of roughly equal to human ability emerge (simplified definition!).

What surprised me is that a cluster of fans emerged who were startup entrepreneurs, venture capitalists, and technologists. It took me a while, but eventually I realized that what this group of people had in common was that they liked to think about the future and technology. When it came to my book, they liked how I depicted the near-term future. They also compared me most often to Daniel Suarez, author of the amazing technothriller *Daemon*.

This caused a shift in how I perceived and marketed my own book. Rather than focusing on reaching out to science fiction reviewers, I reached out to other technologists. Instead of marketing my book to fans of Stross and Doctorow, I marketed to fans of Suarez. I started describing *Avogadro Corp* as a technothriller instead of science-fiction.

As you can see, you may start by anticipating the communities that will be interested in your book, but you should quickly move into discovering which communities actually are most likely to discuss it.

Engaging

What does it mean to engage in a community? When is it acceptable to mention your book? What's the point of it all?

Every community, whether online or offline, is different. I'm a member of a many different online communities, including a college alumni group, two different writer's organizations, several LinkedIn groups about either writing or science fiction, several Reddit groups about writing or science fiction, and an active commenter on several blogs.

Each of those groups has different norms. In the college alumni group, for example, we commonly expect to help each other out professionally. Recent posts include a request for employment, request for feedback on a proposed product, and a request for help with a business plan. So I judged that it would be acceptable in that environment to mentioning publishing my book. Of course, that couldn't be my only contribution to the group. I gave feedback on the product and forwarded announcements.

Good communities are characterized by both give and take.

In most of the writing groups I participate in, a certain amount of promoting your own book is expected and acceptable: when you introduce yourself to the group, and when you publish. But if you only talk about yourself, you'll quickly become tiresome to the group, and they'll quickly ignore your posts.

Other groups, such as genre fan forums, may be a target of frequent self-promotion posts, and so they may have a complete ban on such promotion, or they may relegate it to a particular sub-area. Even if they don't have an explicit policy against it, it may be against etiquette to make self-promotional posts.

These groups can still be very worthwhile communities to engage in, just not in a self-promotional way. You can learn from the community, and contribute to the community. If you're someone who makes frequent, valued contributions to the community, you'll be regarded highly. Even if you never make a self-promotional post, you'll still create a positive reputation for yourself that will, in time, lead to other members of the community who will post about your books.

Every community has different norms, so it's not possible to describe them all here. In general, it's good to participate in a community for a while, several weeks at least, to discover what's acceptable. By then you'll know if the community is right for you, and what degree of self-promotion, if any, is accepted.

Aside from looking for forums or discussion groups on the web, there are other, less obvious ways to engage with communities on the Internet:

- **Post comments on blogs:** Many blogs have established readers or fans. Every time you post a comment, you're engaging with the author of that blog and the entire community of readers. You can revisit blogs you like frequently or subscribe by using an RSS reader. If you contribute valuable comments regularly, you're likely to develop relationships with the author and other readers, some of whom will, in turn, be bloggers. They might even ask you to expand on your comments by writing a guest post, as happened to me when I posted on the IEEE Spectrum Robotics blog. I was subsequently asked to write a guest post about the impact of open source on the future of robotics and artificial intelligence.

- **Post on your own blog:** By posting regularly on your own blog, you can develop your own community or attract the notice of a community. For example, in 2011 I wrote a series of blog posts about Tim Ferriss's *4 Hour Body*, starting with a cheat sheet that put of all of Tim's weight loss tips in a single chart. The community of *4-Hour Body* readers, on their own blogs and in forums, discovered the cheat sheet and other posts, and linked to my blog many dozens of times driving thousands of visits to my blog. The content was so valuable to so many visitors, I ultimately wrote a book called *Slow Carb Fat Loss* that was a compendium of my blog posts on the topic.

- **Tweet and retweet:** Although Twitter may look like individuals acting independently, communities may form around ad-hoc interests indicated through hashtags (those #topic tags that have permeated most social networks now) or around major influencers. Ben Huh is the CEO of Cheezburger and has ten thousand followers on Twitter. One day he tweeted about a topic, I replied, and then another of Ben's followers replied back, and so we had an ongoing stream of discussion around new technology products that had brought in a few other influential members of the tech community on Twitter, and which was visible to many thousands of people. It was a community for only a few dozen minutes, but it was highly visible for that span of time. These kinds of interactions are wonderful ways to meet people and get visibility, but they require a certain kind of comfortable fluency with the medium. That's why I recommend getting started on platforms like Twitter long before you publish.

Bufferapp

All this connecting and social media stuff is fun, but, at the end of the day, writers need to write. The best way I've found to achieve that is to decide, each time I sit down at the computer, whether I'm sitting down to write, or sitting down to engage in social media. I avoid mixing the two, otherwise it becomes too easy to squander my limited and valuable writing time on more social media.

One technique I use is to spend my mornings on writing (when my brain is fresh and creative) and focus a few evenings a week on social media. The downside of this is that I might post a dozen things on Twitter on Sunday night (overwhelming anyone who is listening to me) then be completely absent for days.

To avoid this, I use buffer (http://bufferapp.com). Buffer allows you to create a queue of messages to be posted according to a schedule you define. For example, I have buffer set up to post up to three times per day: once at 9am, once at 11:30, and once at 4pm.

On Sunday night, I might browse a weekends worth of social media sites looking for the latest relevant news articles, videos, or tweets. Then I add those to buffer, and buffer slowly trickles them out over the next few days.

Buffer also lets you post simultaneously to Twitter, your Facebook page, and LinkedIn, covering all of the major social media networks (except Google Plus) in one swoop. Buffer also lets you know how many people clicked on your links and how many reshared your posts.

It's a great time saver, enhances your online presence, and gives you great analytics. I highly recommend it.

Monthly Emails

So you signed up for MailChimp or another mailing list service, and you're ready to start sending emails to the folks who have joined your mailing list. What might you send?

A typical monthly update email for me includes:

- What I'm up to this month in the writing world: writing, editing, sending to publishers, etc.
- Noteworthy accomplishments or accolades for my books. In the beginning, this might just be a really nice review on Amazon, but over time I was able to add blurbs from recognizable influencers, awards that I won, or hitting a new high on a bestseller list.
- Reviews and endorsements of especially good books I've read.
- A call to action, such as asking readers to write a review, tell a friend, buy the next book, etc.

Here are two representative emails I've sent in the past. The initial email was the very first one I sent, about one month after I published *Avogadro Corp*.

Thanks

I want to start by saying thank you to everyone who has helped *Avogadro Corp* get off to such an awesome start. Thanks to you, *Avogadro Corp* is averaging 5 star reviews on Amazon, has shown up on dozens of Goodreads lists, and is available at Powells.com. At the book launch party in December, I signed about twenty copies. And *Silicon Florist*, a prominent

Portland tech blog, published a very nice review. Without friends and readers like you, none of this would have been possible. Thank you.

What's Next

On a writing front, the second book in the series, *A.I. Apocalypse*, is finished, and I'm currently submitting it to literary agents. *A.I. Apocalypse* is also a techno-thriller, and it's set ten years after the events in *Avogadro Corp*. It's an independent story that carries over a few characters. In the story, Leon Tsarev, a teenager from Brooklyn, New York, is coerced by his uncle into writing a computer virus. Leon knows nothing about computer viruses, but he knows a lot about evolutionary biology. He writes a virus that rapidly evolves, developing an entire sentient AI civilization within days. Unfortunately, it causes a collapse of all computers, from cars and phones to payment systems and emergency services. As they flee a burning New York City, Leon knows he has to do something to stop the virus.

I'm also speaking at *SXSW Interactive*, the enormous social media/tech conference, in March. I've proposed a panel called "Wall-E or Terminator: Predicting the Rise of AI". Daniel H. Wilson, author of *Robopocalypse*, and Chris Robson, a brilliant computer scientist whose been studying the nature of conscious as a side project for ten years, will also be on the panel. If you're at *SXSW*, please attend our panel on Tuesday.

Now what?

I don't have a big marketing department or budget like traditional publishers do, so I continue to work on promoting *Avogadro Corp*, and, as always, appreciate any help you contribute.

I've sent out review copies to many dozens of newspapers and bloggers. If you know of someone in media who might like a review copy, please let me know.

Several people have voted for *Avogadro Corp* in Powell's Puddly Awards contest, which ends on January 31st. If you'd be willing to cast your vote too, it would help *Avogadro* get a little local love. Just follow the instructions to submit a customer comment and be sure to click the checkbox for the Puddly award.

Reviews on Amazon and Goodreads help drive sales (as does adding *Avogadro Corp* to lists on Goodreads). And, of course, there's always that old fashioned approach of just telling a friend.

Looking for something to read?

I recently read *The Automatic Detective* by A. Lee Martinez. Described as a mish-mash of science fiction and hard-boiled detective novel, it follows the adventures of a reformed killer robot who drives a taxi and gets embroiled in solving a series of mysteries and murders against his will.

I'm looking forward to reading *Amped* by Daniel Wilson, and preordered it a few days ago.

Until next time,

William Hertling

Here's another example. This one was from June. I had just released my second novel. Notice the prize I offered: a short story I hadn't published, which was the original opening to my third novel, *The Last Firewall*, before I changed direction.

A.I. Apocalypse in Print

I have a short update this month. First off, A.I. Apocalypse is finally available in print! (This is in addition to the Kindle version that's been out for a few months.) This is always exciting, because as nice as ereaders are, it's still fun to hold a book in your hands.

If you or any family members or friends would like the paperback, buy a copy from Amazon.

(Keep reading this email to find out how to get a secret bonus chapter.)

Recommended Books (& Short Short Stories)

I just finished *The Killing Star* by Charles Pellegrino and George Zebrowski. This is definitely a thinking person's science fiction novel. It explores a possible reason why we don't see signs of intelligence life in the universe and makes the case that this is because the best defense against a potentially hostile alien race is a preemptive elimination of that race. Therefore, when a civilization gives off detectable signs of advanced technology (radio waves, for example), the best course of action is to accelerate missiles to near light speed and bomb the planet. Did I mention it makes a very compelling argument? Scary. (This book is out-of-print and not available for Kindle, so you'll need to get a used paperback. Well worth the effort through.)

This month I also re-read *Snow Crash* by Neal Stephenson. Alongside William Gibson's early cyberpunk books and Walter Jon William's

Hardwired, Snow Crash is another of the genre-defining cyberpunk works. I haven't read it in quite a few years, and I was surprised at all the ways I found that it had influenced me.

I also read Daniel H. Wilson's new novel *Amped*. I've posted a full review on my blog. Check it out.

If you like short stories and especially short short stories, please take a look at Bruce Holland Rogers's website shortshortshort.com. Bruce is a masterful short story writer as well as a creative writer professor who teaches both here in the States and abroad. He offers a great subscription model where, for just $10 a year, he emails you three original short stories per month. As he points out, that's less than thirty cents a story. I've just subscribed, and I'm eagerly looking forward to the first installment.

Until Next Time

I'll be working on editing *The Last Firewall* over the next couple of months. I've also written a short story called "Driving Home" that I'll be playing with. It's the first short story I've written (at least since I was a child), so I'm interested in experimenting with the form.

Please post an Amazon review for *A.I. Apocalypse*, if you like it. Reviews are the single best mechanism to enable sales for independent authors. By posting a review, you're a patron of the arts! (Plus they need only to be a single sentence or two and a star rating, and only take a few minutes. Easy-peasy!)

Special offer: The Secret Bonus Chapter. If you post a review and email me with the link, I'll email you back a non-canonical single chapter detailing events that take place after the end of *A.I. Apocalypse* that won't appear in print anywhere else. Just send an email to me with the subject line "Review posted" and a link to your review.[1]

Have a great summer!

William Hertling

---

[1] I've since learned that Amazon doesn't allow you to offer anything in consideration for a review except for a free copy of the product. However, you could use this same idea and apply it to something else, such as a blog post about your book or mentioning it on Twitter.

Facebook Marketing

About six weeks after my initial launch, I decided to experiment with Facebook advertising.

I had used Facebook ads once before, when launching a new web application. I liked Facebook's ability to select which users would see the ad. It's possible to choose based on location, age, and gender, as well as by a person's interests (e.g. the books, authors, movies, or hobbies they've listed in their profile.)

Before I talk about using Facebook ads for books, I want to introduce several concepts: pay-per-click, conversion rates, profitability of ads.

Background

In the old days of newspaper ads, advertisers paid based on how many people would see the ad: a newspaper with a circulation of one million could demand a higher cost per ad space than a newspaper with a circulation of one hundred thousand. But since the advent of the web and the ability to measure when people click on an advertisement, the prevailing and more useful model is **pay-per-click**. The advertiser pays not to place an ad, but when a would-be customer clicks on the ad. Most ad systems are based on bids for position. If one advertiser is willing to pay 80 cents per click, their ads will be shown before another person who is willing to pay 50 cents per click. In most cases, and at the current time (mid-2012), you can expect to pay in the range of 50 cents to one dollar per click for the most likely places an author would like to place an ad.

Conversion rate is the calculation of how many people bought your book after clicking on the advertisement. If twenty people buy your book out of one hundred who click on the advertisement, then the conversion rate is 20%.

Conversion depends on many factors:

1. Does the ad accurately represent the product being sold? There are many gimmicks that can help an ad receive more clicks (promising something free, photos of attractive people). However, if the result is that people are clicking on the ad, but

don't want the product, then the money the advertiser has paid is wasted.

2. Does the landing page (the destination where the ad brings a visitor) make a compelling case for purchasing the book? As I mentioned in the section on book landing pages (see Phase 1), my experiments demonstrated that, in my case, I converted twice as many visitors into book sales when I directed people to my custom book landing page as compared to directing them to my Amazon page.

3. Have you accurately targeted the right customers? I knew that my writing was similar in style and topic matter to Charles Stross, Cory Doctorow, and Daniel Suarez, so I used Facebook's ad filtering tools to choose fans of those writers.

Conversion rates vary, but what really matters for an effective advertising campaign is **profitable advertising**. In general, the cost of advertising should be less than the profit derived from sales. For example, if you spend fifty cents every time someone clicks on an advertisement, but only one out of ten people who click on the ad buy the book, then the advertising cost is $5.00 (50 cents times 10 people). If the profit per book is $2.00, then advertising is not a long-term, cost effective strategy. But, if one out of three people who click on the ad buy the book, then the cost is $1.50, and you're making money with each book sale.

Estimating conversion

Estimating the conversion rate (and hence advertising cost per book sold) is not easy when it comes to books. In virtually all cases, the actual book buying occurs on a third party site (e.g. Amazon, Barnes and Nobles, or Smashwords), and there are no metrics that show how many customers who bought books came from your advertisement.

Here's the technique I used to estimate conversion:

1. After I finished my flurry of initial book launch activity in the first thirty days, my sales began to settle into something of a steady-state. Day-by-day sales fluctuated a little, but they mostly conformed to a weekly cycle. For my books, on

Amazon, barring any external events (like blog reviews), the weekly cycle looks something like this:

- Sales are highest on Saturday and Sunday
- Sales are about 20% lower on Fridays
- Sales are about 30% lower on Mondays
- Sales are about 50% lower on Tuesdays, Wednesdays, and Thursdays

2. Because of this variability, I knew that I couldn't measure the effectiveness of ads on a day-by-day basis. Instead, I kept track of the number of books sold over two weeks and divided by fourteen days to establish my daily sales rate, which was about four books per day. This was my baseline. Unless any external events occurred (e.g. any extensive social media promotion, mentions by other bloggers, etc.), I expect my sales to continue roughly at the same volume.

3. I started my advertising campaign. I ran the campaign for a week. The advertising website (which was Facebook in my case, although this technique would work for any advertising site) gave me statistics for how many people clicked on my ads.

4. At the end of the week, I looked at how many people had purchased my book: forty-nine. I subtracted my baseline: forty-nine books sold, minus the twenty-eight books I expected to sell without advertising, leaves twenty-one books sold, presumably due to advertising.
   Formula: (books sold) − (expected books sold) = (incremental sales due to advertising)

5. Using Twitter search, and Google searches by time, I checked that there were no external events that would have account for the change in sales. I found none. Therefore, my estimate was that twenty-one people purchased my book as a result of the ad. Had there been any external events, I would have had to restart the process by calculating a baseline all over again.

6. I paid an average of forty-five cents each for eighty-four people to click on the advertisement. My conversion rate was 25% (21 purchases divided by 84 ad clicks), and my advertising cost per

book was $1.80 ($0.45 per ad * 84 clicks / 21 sales).

Formulas:

(incremental sales) / (ad clicks) = (conversion rate)

(cost per click) * (ad clicks) / (incremental sales) = (cost per book sold)

Negative return advertising

Even when the return on advertising is negative (the cost of advertising is more than the profit made per book), there are still times when it makes sense to advertise. If you need to kick-start purchases and reviews because no one knows about the book, then it's worth getting the word out, even if it costs you more than you make. If you are trying to break into a bestseller list, and sales of the book are close, but not quite enough, then advertising might be called for. In either case, it's a temporary strategy to be employed for a few days or weeks, but not long-term.

Positive return advertising

When the return is positive (the profit is more than the cost of ads), then advertising makes sense as a long-term strategy. You can continue to advertise indefinitely, knowing that every ad is generating more profit than its cost. You may also be able to scale your advertising spend. In other words, if you've set a spending budget of five dollars per day, and it's profitable, you test spending ten dollars per day. You will need to calculate the conversion rate again at this higher level to know if the advertising still generates a profit. If so, you can raise the amount you're spending further and then test again.

At a certain point, you will saturate your target market. That is, your ads are reaching everyone they can reach, and no further spending will increase the number of books purchased.

Eventually, you will pass the point of saturation. Not only have you reach everyone who is a potential buyer, you've already sold them all books. At this point, the return on advertising begins to decrease because you're paying to show ads to people to who are unlucky to buy even if they click on the ad. At this point, it makes sense to scale back or stop advertising, or find new targeted markets to go after.

How To Create a Campaign

If you haven't advertised on Facebook before, here's a quick overview. The process is fairly self-explanatory once you understand the basic concept.

1. Go to http://facebook.com/ads or click on the advertising link at the bottom of the main Facebook page.
2. Ads consist of an image, a title, a small amount of text, and a destination link.
3. You pay per click, so it only costs you when someone clicks on the advertisement. Ads can be targeted by age, sex, country, region, and interests.
4. You can set spending limits so you're in control of how much you spend. You can conduct a useful ad experiment with as little as twenty dollars.

I knew my own writing would appeal to fans of Charles Stross, Cory Doctorow, and William Gibson. I write about similar subjects in a similar style. Therefore I ran a series of Facebook ads specifically targeting fans of each of those authors.

Facebook's advertising console tells me how much I'm paying per click. For example, in the last seven days, I had 96 clicks on my Charles Stross targeted ad, and paid $0.34 per click.

The advertising console also tells me the CTR (click through rate).

A typical Facebook ad

For my author-specific ads, the CTR has been 0.2% and higher. That tells me that out of every 1,000 times the ad has been shown, it's been clicked on two times. That might not sound very high, but compared to loosely targeted ads (e.g. people who like read, or people who live in a certain geography), it's anywhere from ten to a hundred times higher than those more general ads.

In Facebook, you define campaigns and ads:

- A campaign has a budget (e.g. $10/day or $100 total) and a time limit (e.g. Run my ads from September 1st through 15th.)
- An ad has specific text, image, and destination that creates what is displayed, plus targeting that selects who will see the ad.
- You can run multiple ads within a campaign, and Facebook will automatically rotate between ads, finding the ads that generate the most traffic.
- It's normal to create many different ads as you experiment to find what text and images work best.

The URL for a Facebook ad can be any page on the Internet or your Facebook author page. As I mentioned, for my first novel, I directed people to avogadrocorp.com. For my second novel, I switched to a subpage off my main site (http://www.williamhertling.com/p/ai-apocalypse.html). I'm specifically trying to drive sales of the book, as opposed to getting people to follow me or any other objective. You could also send people directly to an Amazon.com page for your book, but I prefer that the URL in the ad also reflects my book's brand, and, as I mentioned in the section on book landing pages, my experiments show that nearly twice as many sales result when I sent people to my book's landing page.

Goodreads

Goodreads describes themselves as "the world's largest site for readers and book reviews". I signed up for Goodreads to check it out, and filled out my author page and claimed my books. One thing I've noticed about Goodreads is that users are very active. They may rate, review, or update status on dozens of books each and every month. Because Goodreads users are so passionate about reading, this is a great place to spend time.

The main things I did:

- Claim my author page, fill out details, and link to my blog.
- Go over the entries for my books, filling in any missing details or extras.
- Set up a Goodreads advertising campaign.
- Set up a Goodreads Giveaway.

I'll cover each of these in a little more detail. The entry point for all of these activities is via the Goodreads Author Program: http://www.goodreads.com/author/program.

Author Page

The Goodreads Author profile allows you to set up your name, photo, biography, list influencers, and link to your official website and Twitter profile. You can also share your favorite books and recent

Goodreads author profile page

reads, promote upcoming events (such as a book signing), share excerpts, etc.

Start by signing up for Goodreads, then search for your published name on the site. Then click "Is this you?" to send a request to join the Author program.

Book Details

Search for your book on Goodreads using the search box in the upper left hand corner of the site. If your book is already listed, check that the information is accurate and sufficient. If it's not listed, the search results will include a button for "Still can't find the book? Add a new record." Follow this path to enter all the necessary data.

Remember to upload a photograph of the book cover!

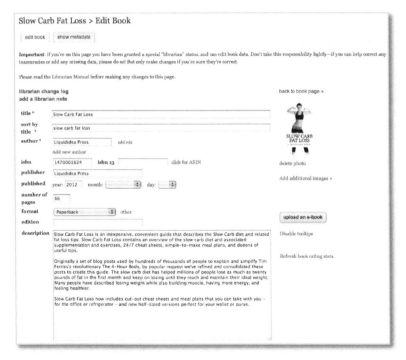

Data entry for book listing on Goodreads

Lists

One of Goodreads most popular features is Listopia, their user generated book lists. Anyone can create a list, and once created, anyone else can vote for books on the list. Since many readers will browse lists looking for new books, this is an ideal opportunity to get additional exposure for your book.

The trick lies in figuring out the right lists for your book, especially if you aren't a frequent Goodreads user. I wasn't aware of Goodreads lists until I noticed a few of the more enthusiastic readers of my first

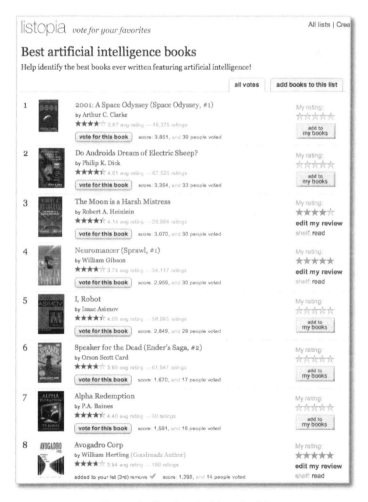

Example Goodreads Listopia List

book had added it to many different lists. They voted to add it to lists such as "Best science fiction novels" or "Best science fiction novels of 2011." These were wonderful endorsements, but it's difficult for a book to get into a notable placement on such lists, because the lists themselves are so popular. If the top ten books all have hundreds or thousands of votes, and even the hundredth book has twenty votes, these are good signs that it would be very hard to break into the list, just as its very hard to break onto the New York Times bestseller list.

After some searching I found lists such as "Best artificial intelligence books" and "Best novels with a computer character". These lists were very relevant and much easier to break into. When you find a relevant list, use the "Add books to this list" link to vote for your own books.

Goodreads Advertising

Because Goodreads attracts so many readers, it seems like a no-brainer to invest in advertising there. I originally thought that, like Facebook advertising, I'd be able to measure the conversion rate for my Goodreads ads.

Surprisingly, many people saw my Goodreads advertisement (up to several thousand a day), but very few clicked on the ad. In most cases, this is a sign that there's something wrong with the advertisement. However, I was already investing a lot of effort in my Facebook advertising strategy, and I just didn't have the time to experiment with my Goodreads ad.

Of the $100 I seeded my Goodreads ad campaign with, I still have $80 left six months later. Meanwhile, many tens of thousands of people have seen my ad. I decided that the Goodreads ad was a nice way to create impressions (the number of times people see an ad) at relatively low cost. That's a different strategy than my Facebook advertising campaign, where my goal has been to drive profitable conversions.

But it turns out that Goodreads offers an even more effective way to reach would-be readers: the Goodreads Giveaway.

Goodreads Giveaway

The Goodreads Giveaway is a fantastic way to reach a large number of readers very inexpensively. A giveaway is essentially a mini-contest administered by Goodreads, in which the prize is a free book. As an author, you describe the book, choose how many books you're willing to give away, and schedule the giveaway.

I offered my second book, *A.I. Apocalypse*, in a giveaway on Goodreads in June. The giveaway was open for three weeks, and more than eight hundred people entered to win one of eight copies. When the contest was over, Goodreads emailed me the list of the eight winners, and I mailed the winners their books.

The giveaway is wonderful in two ways. First, a relatively high proportion of giveaway winners (about 20% in my experience) post a review, either on Goodreads or on Amazon. Second, every one of the more than eight hundred winners gets *A.I. Apocalypse* automatically entered into their own "to-read" list when the giveaway ends. Since many Goodreads readers use their "to-read" list as a queue of books they want to read, this sets up the opportunity for many future sales.

Create a giveaway at http://www.goodreads.com/giveaway/new.

Phase 3 Checklist

- ☐ Monitor mentions and inbound links
- ☐ Engage with fans
- ☐ Connect with communities
- ☐ Participate on social networks
  - ☐ Optional: Schedule posts with Bufferapp
- ☐ Continue blogging
- ☐ Send monthly emails using mailing list
- ☐ Use targeted facebook ads
  - ☐ Monitor results for effectiveness
- ☐ Add to Listopia lists on Goodreads
- ☐ Conduct Goodreads Giveaway

Phase 4: Influencers

Introduction

In this section, I'm going to talk about several interrelated topics: influencers, manufacturing serendipity, the favor economy, and touching on contemporary issues.

Influencers are the people who, because of their experience, reputation or knowledge command a high degree of loyalty from a particular group of people. Manufacturing serendipity synchronicity is the idea that we can improve the probability of something good happening. The favor economy is the notion that people are motivated more by receiving and giving help than by money or fame. Touching contemporary issues is the idea that writing can be more than a good story; it can touch on broader issues that motivate interest.

These interrelated ideas will combine to give you the most powerful tool of all to drive sales.

I'll start by telling a story.

By February, about three months after I had released my book, I was selling about eight books per day. I had already sold several hundred copies. It felt wonderful to have steady sales, fan email from readers, and good ratings on Amazon.

But my dream was to become a full-time writer. With several kids and family obligations, I needed to earn as much from writing as I earned as a software engineer, before I would be able to afford to leave my day job. That meant I needed to sell many more books than I was currently selling.

One Saturday morning in mid-February, I was online and saw something I'd never seen before: a popup from a service I used called bit.ly, alerting me that a large number of people were clicking on my links. (If you don't know what bit.ly is, it's one of several URL shortening services people using to make smaller and/or customized URLs. Besides making the URLs shorter or more readable, bitly also gives you statistics about how many people have clicked on the links. It's a valuable tool to have in your arsenal.)

I couldn't imagine what was causing this sudden uptick. I searched for my book by title on Google, filtering for only those results in the last 24 hours. I found that a man named Brad Feld had written a blog post mentioning and endorsing *Avogadro Corp*. In fact, as I dug around further, I realized that he hadn't just written about my book on his blog, he'd also spoken about it at a talk he'd given and posted reviews on Amazon and Goodreads.

Brad Feld turned out to be a venture capitalist who was a cofounder of TechStars and a director of The Foundry Group. He had more than 100,000 Twitter followers, many fans of his blog, and his blog content was syndicated across many different web sites.

In one day, I sold more than a hundred copies. My book rose through the Amazon ranks, hitting both the Technothriller and High Tech Science Fiction bestseller lists. More people tweeted about it. As the days passed by, sales continued at about three times the rate they'd been before, and some of those new readers posted their own reviews and blog posts that kept the momentum going. From that day forward, *Avogadro Corp* stayed in the top 100 bestselling books in both categories.

But the story doesn't end there. Thanks to a relationship I developed with Brad Feld, he posted a guest blog post I wrote and posted a review of my second book a few months later. This drove yet more sales and helped kick in the Amazon recommendation engine in a big way. Suddenly, my books were being recommended on other bestselling authors' book pages. *Avogadro Corp* hit the #2 bestselling technothriller while *A.I. Apocalypse* hit the #5 spot.

They've since received endorsements from other influencers, and sales have continued near these levels.

While I haven't quit my day job yet, my royalties now allow me to work part-time. I'm closer to realizing my dream of being a full-time writer.

As I'll explain, this story demonstrates the influencer effect, the principle of manufacturing luck, the favor economy, and the relevance of contemporary issues.

Influencer Effect

Writing and publishing a book doesn't guarantee any sales. Many authors write good, even great novels, and then limp along, selling a few books a week. Daniel Suarez's *Daemon*, a fantastic technothriller, started life as a self-published book selling fifty copies a month.

But one day, Rick Klau, a prominent member of the technology community, happen to read *Daemon*, and thought it was an incredible book that should reach a larger audience. He started by writing a review of *Daemon*, then used his connections to help Suarez get the book out to more people:

> "Soon after my review, Dan and I began swapping e-mails and became friends. I introduced him to some other folks who I thought would like the book - and each time, their reaction was the same as mine: Where'd this guy come from? And how can we help?
>
> Eric Olson loved it, and got copies to give out at Tech Cocktail. Steven Vore loved it. CC Chapman loved it. Jim McGee loved it. Matt Cutts loved it, leading to a number of his readers to buy copies and tell their friends. John Robb loved it, and introduced Dan to a few of his friends. Craig Newmark loved it and gave Dan a blurb for promotional materials. Somewhere in all of this, after a few months,

things started to snowball. I shared it with a number of co-workers at Google, where it became something of an underground hit - I know of several dozen now who've read the book and swear by it."[2]

Due in large part to Rick Klau's influence and connections, Suarez went on to get a traditional publishing deal for *Daemon*, and it was relaunched with broad distribution and a big budget advertising campaign. Suarez was able to leave his day job and become a full-time writer.

Influencers like Rick Klau and Brad Feld play an increasingly significant role in the attention received by products of any kind, including books. Tim Ferriss believes that single author blogs (e.g. blogs that are written by one person who has a loyal following) are the most important tool for getting new products adopted. Michael Ellsberg wrote about the Tim Ferriss effect:

"There's a big difference between being exposed to a large audience, and being exposed to a comparatively smaller (but still large) audience which is ridiculously passionate.

The former is very nice; the latter is priceless.

You know the oft-observed phenonmenon in politics, that a passionate minority can have influence far beyond a diffuse, apathetic majority?

That is the essence of the Tim Ferriss Effect--which goes way beyond Tim Ferriss. It's better to be exposed to a comparatively smaller group of people who are engaged, devoted and passionate, than to a much larger group of people who are casual readers."[3]

Mass media can address a larger audience, but we're less likely to be influenced by an unknown reviewer in the *New York Times* or on a book review blog. Friend's opinions may mean a lot to us, especially if they have expertise and a record of good recommendations in a given area, but the reach of the average person is small. Influencers fall somewhere in between: we feel a connection with them because it's a single person who we've followed over some time, and their credibility

---

[2] Source: http://tins.rklau.com/2009/01/daemon-is-about-to-be-bestseller.html
[3] Source: http://www.forbes.com/sites/michaelellsberg/2012/01/11/the-tim-ferriss-effect/

is high because they're almost certainly an expert in their area, and their reach is large enough to have a significant impact.

Making Luck

Many people who achieve a breakout experience, whether it's landing an agent, getting a publisher, or having a bestseller, will recount how lucky they were to accomplish what they did. Chance does indeed play a big role: the right meeting with the right person at the right time isn't something you can guarantee.

But it is possible to manufacture luck. Some called this planned serendipity. You foster conditions that create an environment that will enable meeting the right person at the right time.

Let's take a simple example. Let's say you want to meet a famous movie star. If you stay in your home, it's extremely unlikely that a famous movie star will come knocking on your door. If you're out and about in a small city, the odds are still small. If you go to a bigger city, the odds increase. But, if you spend a year in Hollywood, the odds are very high that you'll meet a famous movie star.

Let's take a step back and look at the role of Phase 1, 2, and 3 activities in manufacturing serendipity.

The techniques described in this book should help you achieve a burst of initial sales, use those sales to generate reviews, mentions in social media, and entries in Amazon's recommendation engine. All of those should help you rise above the noise level of the hundreds of thousands of other publications and have a modest number of ongoing sales.

However, they won't, by themselves, achieve a breakthrough bestseller. I did those steps, and I was selling three hundred books a month. Those are respectable sales, but they aren't sufficient to support full-time writing.

But those sales and mentions set up the conditions for luck: with enough people reading it, the odds are better that someone who is an influencer will come across it; either reading the book itself, or reading some of the social media mention. If an influencer like Brad Feld or

Rick Klau becomes interested, they'll have a dramatic effect that can lead to bestseller level sales.

In addition, those initial reviews and sales establish a minimum level of credibility that makes it easier for an influencer to decide if a book is worth their time. In fact, the effect builds: once you have an endorsement from one influencer, it's easier to get other influencers to also take a look.

If you have the connections to reach directly to influencers, then by all means, take advantage of that as early as possible. But if you don't, then your initial sales will set up the conditions that increase the likelihood of making those connections.

Touching on contemporary issues

When I first published, I imagined that the people who would be most interested in my books would have something in common. I guessed that would be an interest in the technological singularity (the point at which computers become smarter than humans, leading to a runaway artificial intelligence explosion), or an interest in the same authors I read (Cory Doctorow, Charles Stross, etc.)

After Brad Feld recommended *Avogadro Corp*, several other technology luminaries also recommended it, including Ben Huh (CEO of Cheezburger), Amber Case (cyborg anthropologist and TED speaker), and others.

I found myself wondering what these people had in common. They didn't outwardly appear to have a high interest in the singularity. At least, it wasn't something they talked about often.[4] They didn't seem to share an interest in the same authors as far as I could tell. I even joked with a friend: "I'm huge with venture capitalists."

It took me about a month of puzzling over this before it hit me: technology leaders have a common interest in understanding the future of technology. They want to know and think about where

---

[4] How did I discover what they talked about? I followed them on Twitter and read their blog posts. This is another example of why it's important to become conversant with social media tools before you need to use them for a critical engagement.

technology is going in five, ten or twenty years. My books are all about technology: where it's going, how it affects society, and how progress in one area affects other areas.

This realization brought me back to a commonly held belief among authors: It's easier to market non-fiction books than fiction books. Non-fiction books are about topics (e.g. how to train your dog), and potential readers search for non-fiction books by topic. They'll enter "training dogs" into Google or Amazon, and if it shows up in the list, they'll consider it. Or they'll read a blog about training dogs, and that blog might mention a book on training dogs.

By comparison, few people search for fiction books by topic. Readers don't, by in large, think "I'd like to read a book about dwarves and elves set in a mystical land involving a magical ring," and then set out to search for "dwarves elves magical rings." They might think, more broadly, "I'd like to read fantasy," but that's so generic as to be impossible to get your book to show up in the search results.

There are usually larger numbers of people passionate about real-world issues than about specific microgenres of fiction. There are more people interested in dog training and sharing information about it than there are people interested in near-term artificial intelligence thrillers and writing blogs about that.

The challenge for fiction writers is to figure out what contemporary, real-life issues are part of their book and would be of potential interest to the world at large. For my writing, it turned out that the contemporary issue I addressed is predicting the future of technology, in general, and artificial intelligence, in particular.

Emlyn Chand wrote *Farsighted*, a fantasy novel whose protagonist is blind. Sherwood Smith and Rachel Manija wrote *Stranger*, a young-adult novel whose protagonist is gay. Marni Bates wrote a young-adult novel that revolved around the effect that social media could have on a girl entering a new school.

These novels are all still stories, first and foremost, but they touch on real-life issues that engage readers and especially influencers.

If you can make this connection to real-life issues and are ready to discuss it and build on it, this will greatly increase the exposure you'll get.

Building Relationships

Learning just one principle will make you more successful when connecting with influencers, whether you initiate the contact or they do. The principle is "give, give, give, ask." Let me explain.

Reciprocity is a psychological principle that in response to friendly actions, people respond in a cooperative, nice manner, more so than would be dictated by simple self-interest. (The corollary is true: in response to hostile actions, people respond in a hostile fashion.)

The classic psychological study on reciprocity is *Effects of a favor and liking on compliance* by Dennis T. Regan at Cornell University:

> A laboratory experiment was conducted to examine the effects of a favor and of liking on compliance with a request for assistance from a confederate. Liking for the confederate was manipulated, and male subjects then received a soft drink from the confederate, from the experimenter, or received no favor. Compliance with the confederate's request to purchase some raffle tickets was measured, as was liking for the confederate. The results showed that the favor increased liking for the confederate and compliance with his request, but the effect of manipulated liking was weak. Detailed ratings of the confederate as well as correlational data suggested that the relationship between favors and compliance is mediated, not by liking for the favor-doer, but by normative pressure to reciprocate.[5]

In plain English, the experiment measured the effect of giving a soda to someone and then asking them to buy raffle tickets. Those people who received the soda, even though they hadn't asked for one, bought more tickets on average than those who did not receive the favor.

---

[5] Source: Regan, R. T. (1971). "Effects of a favor and liking on compliance". Journal of Experimental Social Psychology 7: 627-639.
http://dx.doi.org/10.1016/0022-1031(71)90025-4

But there are limits to reciprocity. One small favor does not make a relationship where there wasn't one before. And asking for something too big too early can sour a relationship.

David Siteman Garland, author of *Smarter, Faster, Cheaper* wrote an article about building relationships: *From Tim Ferriss to Seth Godin: How to Interview and Build Relationships with the Most "Influential" People in the World*. You can find it at http://bit.ly/favoreconomy. He writes that the most important principle of the favor economy is to "ask for nothing":

#3: ASK FOR NOTHING

Number three on the list is the secret sauce that most people forget. By doing it, scarily, you will separate yourself from 98% of the pack.

Because, most people in that initial contact add step #5 (which is to ask for something). That might be something like: "Can you RT this?" or "Hey can I interview you now on my show?"

Yuck. You are doing something nice. Giving someone a present. Not a Trojan horse with stipulations and requests. Everyone likes their ego stroked a little bit. How can you show some love?

This brings us back to the cadence of "give, give, give, ask." If you can consistently do small favors for people, without expectation of anything in return, they're likely to either reciprocate on their own, or return a favor when you ask for one later.

What can you give as a favor? It depends on the person. David Garland says you could write an article about them, and then send them an email and let them know they're in the article. You can help solve a problem for them, if they tweet or blog about an issue they're having. You can make an introduction for them. Or suggest an improvement to their blog. You can tweet about their big events, such as a new product comes out, or they have an announcement to make. You can leave thoughtful comments on their blog posts.

After Brad Feld wrote a favorable review of *Avogadro Corp*, tripling my rate of sales, my good friend Gene Kim said that I needed to return the favor as a thank you. I couldn't figure out what might be appropriate, and Gene suggested a blog post. I was stymied. What could I write about that would be an appropriate gift?

It took me a month of thinking about it in the back of my mind before I finally connected the dots. As I described earlier, I realized that Brad Feld and the other technologists really liked my novel because it thought about the future. Therefore it made sense that if I could write about the principles I used to predict the future, it would be of interest to him. I sent a short email to the effect of "Thanks again for the review. I wanted to do something to reciprocate. Could I offer you up a blog post? I'm thinking of an article on 'How to Predict the Future.'"

Brad said yes. I wrote the article, laboring over every word to make it as perfect as possible, and, a month later, the post went up. It was good for Brad's blog (the article was retweeted and mentioned several hundred times, and is now the top Google result for "How to Predict the Future").

Shortly after that, Brad reviewed my second book, and doubled all of my sales again.

By the way, if you've been reading carefully, you'll recall that in the Book Launch phase, I recommended that you ask friends and family to buy your book. There was no "give, give, give" prior to the "ask". By definition, you will already have a relationship with your friends and family. Hopefully, you can draw on the strength of that relationship, such that they will be willing to do you the favor of buying your book. If you don't have a relationship with friends and family in which you do favors for each other, it's never too late to start. Give each other rides to the airport, help a friend when they're looking for work or starting a new business, offer to dog-sit or house-watch, or bring them a meal when they're going through a hard time.

Putting It All Together

Now we're going to put all of these together:
1. Make your own luck by getting the initial sales and reviews that will help draw attention to your book and get it into the hands of influencers.

2. If you touch on contemporary, real-life issues, it will increase the likelihood that people will find a deeper connection to what you are writing, and therefore recommend it to others.

3. Make it a habit to do favors for people, to cultivate relationships. Some of those people will be influencers that would be likely to have an interest in your book.

All of these will increase the likelihood of influencers with a big following talking about your book. That can boost you from a steady stream of ongoing sales into bestselling status within your category.

Phase 4 Checklist

- ☐ Look for influencers
- ☐ Make luck (e.g. set yourself up for the conditions that will bring you what you need)
- ☐ Touch on contemporary issues
- ☐ Give, give, give, ask
- ☐ Build relationships

Other Topics

What's Next

Although this is a marketing book, over the long term, your goal as a writer is to spend more time writing and less time marketing.

Indeed, *Not a Gold Rush - The Taleist Self-Publishing Survey*, a survey of more than a thousand indie published authors, found that those who spent the most time writing, as opposed to marketing, earned the most money. (Available on Amazon at http://bit.ly/notagoldrush and well worth the money.)

If you have one book that is selling, releasing a second book is good for several reasons:

1. Each person who buys and enjoys the first book is likely to buy the second book. This alone could double your sales.
2. With two books out, you have twice as many chances to be discovered on book sites, because either book might be found via recommendations and browsing.

You may be wondering: Why not just write and forget about marketing?

Until you break out of the level of noise and develop a readership, additional books won't magically create more sales. If your first book is earning $10,000 a year, then a second book may help you earn $20,000. But if your first book is earning $50 a year, then the second book will only bring you to $100.

Even once you've experienced success, it still makes sense to do marketing for each subsequent book, but the level of investment will be less. Friends and family will be less likely to go all out for subsequent books. You'll already be active on social media and blogging, and so you won't need to increase the effort there, just shift it to the new book. Similarly, instead of creating a website from scratch, you'll just be doing some minor updates to add your new book.

So get off Facebook, stop blogging so much, and go write your next amazing book.

What Didn't Work

It's important to understand when a marketing technique doesn't work. Then you can take a step back to evaluate what's going on.
- Are you doing it wrong?
- Is there something you can do to improve the results you're getting?
- Or, is the technique simply not effective?

When you have limited time or money to put into marketing (and we all do), then quickly identifying what isn't working, and making a course correction is vitally important.

Below I'll share a few techniques that didn't work for me.

Mutual Twitter Following

When I first started learning about book promotion, one thing I found on LinkedIn, Facebook, and other forums were mutual follow lists. It would usually propose something along the lines of "Let's all follow each other on Twitter. Post your twitter handle here."

It seems like an attractive idea. You can easily gain followers and a bigger audience. Then when you launch your new book, some of your followers will buy it. The more followers you have, the thinking goes, the more people who will buy your book.

Or you might be interested in gaining Twitter followers because you're concerned about building reputation and platform. The logic goes something like this: If you have more followers, people will take you seriously. If you have ten thousand followers, publishers and agents will notice you.

Unfortunately, mutual following fails on both accounts.

Here's why:

The people who are following each other on these lists are not your core audience. What they have is common is that they are all self-published authors. They will not buy your young adult urban fantasy romance steampunk crossover novel.

How likely would you be to buy novels in genres you don't read from people you don't know? Not very.

It's different when you have members of a true community. I'm a member of two different writers groups. I follow many of the members on Twitter. I also talk to them online several days a week. I am likely to buy their books. I follow them because I have a genuine interest in them as people and because of the interests we share.

Onto reputation and platform:

A high Twitter follower count, by itself, is not an indicator of reputation or influence. When evaluating a person's Twitter platform, there are two metrics to consider: a high follower-to-following ratio and a high follower count.

Someone who has ten thousand followers, but is also following ten thousand people, gives the appearance of someone who is gaming the system. In other words, roughly equal follower/following counts is a good indicator that the Twitter user is engaging in mutual following to increase their follower count.

By comparison, someone who is followed by two thousand people, but is themselves only following five hundred people, usually has gained followers for a legitimate reason. Usually that reason is because they share interesting insights, have true fans, or influence of some kind.

I recommend you stay away from mutual Twitter following except when you have a real relationship and shared interests with an existing community.

Review Copies for Newspapers

In 2011, about seven hundred thousand books were self-published. If five percent, or thirty-five thousand, are mailed via the postal service, to the *New York Times*, that would be about *one hundred unsolicited books arriving daily* on the desk of the one or two writers they have assigned to book reviews. That would be on top of the five or ten books they're getting from agents and publishers, who serve as something of a buffer for them. The odds of a reviewer picking up your book out of that slush pile is not likely. It's probably all they can do to shove the books into recycling each day.

It's not cheap, either: it costs about five dollars per book to order the book, put it in an envelope, and mail it out.

I did send about a hundred review copies combined for both *Avogadro Corp* and *A.I. Apocalypse*. Even though I focused on newspapers where I thought I had the greatest chance of success (local and community papers where I live and where the books are set), not a single review was printed. It was a tremendous expense of time and money with no effect at all.

Review Copies to Amazon Reviewers

I'd heard that it's possible to browse the top Amazon reviewers, and then ask them to review your book.

It took about twenty hours to comb through the top five hundred Amazon reviewers to find twenty-five who were open to solicitations and interested in science fiction. (If you want to do this, you'll find that the top reviewers usually list their email address and interests in their Amazon profile.)

It took me another ten hours to send each one an individual email, pitching them on why they'd be interested in the book. I send them a .mobi copy of the book, so at least the financial cost was low.

Of those twenty-five people I pitched, I received two reviews. The first review was good. The second review was the only one-star review I received, and it wasn't even accurate: the reviewer found fault primarily with the strongest part of the novel.

In sum, it was a large effort for a tiny number of reviews, and the negative review obviously didn't help.

Unless you're desperate for reviews, I think it's better to wait for organic reviews to trickle in from the people who have a true interest in your book.

Questionable: Award Contests

Some book contests are known as *award farms*. They make their money up front on large entry fees ranging from thirty to sixty dollars. They typically have dozens of categories with several levels of winning within each category. The idea is to give an author the maximum chance of winning. In effect, you're paying for the right to put the words "Winner of the XYZ Award" on your profile.

When I published *Avogadro Corp*, I didn't know about award farms and didn't distinguish them from legitimate contests. I entered eight contests, and won in two of them. I did add text to my Amazon pages and book landing page that I'd won.

I don't know if entering and winning the contests had an effect. I don't think it was harmful. If you recognize award farms for what they are (words you can put on a webpage), then it may be worthwhile.

Real literary contests are distinguished usually by having far fewer awards, a modest entry fee, and will often have a recognizable name.

Never: Pay for Reviews

This is something I don't know much about, except that there was a flurry of discussion and outrage in the blogosphere when it was uncovered that several prominent self-published authors had paid for reviews.

I do not think you should even consider paying for reviews.

First and foremost, if you are writing and publishing, I assume that you have an interest in building a career as a writer. (If your only interest is in making money, there are easier ways to do that.)

You will never have the respect of other writers, agents, publishers, or many readers, if you're found to do something as unethical as paying for reviews.

Second, Amazon and other marketplaces have a vested interest in having the system of peer reviews be useful and meaningful. That means that Amazon will work hard to discover and root out any activity that erodes trust in reviews. In the worst-case scenario, you could be prohibited from selling on Amazon or other sites. Without a marketplace, and, in particular, without Amazon, it will be next to impossible for you to sell books.

Other Resources

- I blog about book marketing, writing, indie publishing and other topics at http://williamhertling.com. Subscribe to my RSS feed or my mailing list for more updates on this and related topics.
- If you'd like to find more time to write and market, learn more about marketing, and generally be more effective with your time, I highly recommend Tim Ferriss's *4-Hour Workweek*.
- Look for writers groups, either online or in your local community. Writers groups can help you learn from more experienced writers, get questions asked, network, and socialize with like-minded people. I'm a member of two groups, one that is heavily focused on indie publishing, and the other more focused on the craft of writing.

Checklists

The following checklists are here to help you put all the steps together in one place. I recommend you photocopy these pages or get a free downloadable PDF version from my website at http://www.williamhertling.com, and then check off items as you go.

Phase 1: Pre-Launch

- [ ] Book Focused
  - [ ] Choose title
  - [ ] Run title effectiveness testing
  - [ ] Get professional cover design
  - [ ] Interior design
  - [ ] Ereader conversion
  - [ ] Include after-matter call to action
- [ ] Web/Social Media
  - [ ] Create book landing page
  - [ ] Establish blog
  - [ ] Write at least five blog posts
  - [ ] Create mailing list
  - [ ] Sign up and use Facebook and Twitter
- [ ] Create and order business cards

Phase 2: Book Launch

- [ ] Time for November/December if possible, otherwise January to April.
- [ ] Simultaneous launch of Kindle/Print formats
- [ ] Week 0   date: _____
  - [ ] Publish
  - [ ] Kindle (allow 48 hours)
  - [ ] Print (allow 1 week)
  - [ ] Ensure print and kindle pages are linked on Amazon
  - [ ] Set up opt-in mailing list (e.g. MailChimp)
  - [ ] Set up Author Central profile and book descriptions
- [ ] Week 1   date: _____
  - [ ] Close friends and family appeal
  - [ ] Learn how to check sales reports
  - [ ] Make follow-up appeal
- [ ] Week 2   date: _____
  - [ ] Wide-spread friends, family, coworker appeal
  - [ ] Follow-up appeal with solicitation to join mailing list
- [ ] Week 3   date: _____

- [ ] Send review copies to influencers
- [ ] Update landing page with testimonials from reviews
- [ ] Use social media to share news, including good reviews, sales milestones, etc.
- [ ] Week 4   date: _____
    - [ ] Hold book launch party

Phase 3: Post-Launch

- [ ] Monitor mentions and inbound links
- [ ] Engage with fans
- [ ] Connect with communities
- [ ] Participate on social networks
    - [ ] Optional: Schedule posts with Bufferapp
- [ ] Continue blogging
- [ ] Send monthly emails using mailing list
- [ ] Use targeted facebook ads
    - [ ] Monitor results for effectiveness
- [ ] Add to Listopia lists on Goodreads
- [ ] Conduct Goodreads Giveaway

Phase 4: Influencers

- [ ] Look for influencers
- [ ] Make luck (e.g. set yourself up for the conditions that will bring you what you need)
- [ ] Touch on contemporary issues
- [ ] Give, give, give, ask
- [ ] Build relationships

Thank You

Thank you for buying and reading *Indie & Small Press Book Marketing*. I hope you find the tips and plans within as useful and effective in building as readership as I did.

As you put this book into practice, if you have a success story you'd like to share, or spot an error, please send me an email at whertling@liquididea.com.

If you enjoyed it, please tell a friend, share via social networks or blogs, or post a review on Amazon or Goodreads.

Sign up for my mailing list at http://williamhertling.com if you'd like more tips on self-publishing, promotion, or to learn when I publish something new.

Thanks,
William Hertling

Acknowledgements

Every book takes a community to publish.

First, I want to thank all the readers of my fiction novels, whose support and enthusiasm made these wonderful experiences happen. This includes some of the big fish so critical to getting the word out: Jason Glaspey, Brad Feld, Ben Huh, and Amber Case.

For inspiration, I'd like to thank Tim Ferriss, Gene Kim, Dave Cornfold and Steven Lewis, as well as the Northwest Independent Writers Association and Codex writers groups.

I'd also like to thank Bainbridge Graduate Institute, where I earned my MBA in sustainable business, and took my first classes on marketing. In particular, I'd like to thank Jill Bamburg, my marketing professor, and Gifford Pinchot, for continual inspiration in the entrepreneurial realm.

For reading and providing feedback, I'd like to thank the Codex community, Tonya Macalino, Erik Wecks, Erin Gately, and Gene Kim.

Bryan Thomas Schmidt provided editing assistance. You can find him at http://bryanthomasschmidt.net if you need an editor. Any errors that remain are my own.

CL Smith provided the cover design. You can get beautiful book covers at http://humblenations.com.

Thanks to Maureen Gately for formatting and design guidance.

Of course, I couldn't do this without the support and patience of Erin and our children. Thank you!

Made in the USA
San Bernardino, CA
03 March 2013